Advance praise for If Not N

'This is the go-to book for an informative, comprehensive and logical approach to career management and job hunting. Its style is extremely accessible, with practical advice clearly illustrated by real-life examples to which one can readily relate. Whether or not you're currently undergoing a career transition, I highly recommend reading this book since it offers thought-provoking ideas and inspiration from two experts in the field.'
Elizabeth Bird, Former MBA Recruitment Manager at Shell

'This is a must-have book. Camilla and Jane are experts in their field and have drawn on their experience to write a practical, straightforward guide whether you are trying to work out your perfect job, going through the job search process or wanting to develop your career.'
Cathy Holley, Partner, Boyden Search Ltd.

'Thoughtful and well structured advice mixed with real-life stories bring the challenges of career choice and change to life. Written from a practitioner's experience of working with diverse talent.'
Elaine Hewens, Interim Head of Learning and Development at Waterstones

'This book will be of huge benefit to people wanting to chart a new direction or take greater control of their career outcomes. The authors have outlined practical steps for identifying options and developing action plans, and it is fantastic to find such comprehensive advice in one volume.'
Susan Gatell, Associate Director, Judge Business School, University of Cambridge

'The good news is that help is at hand. Jane and Camilla have a unique background which puts them in an ideal position to provide sound career advice: they have changed careers themselves, they have been recruiters so they have a solid understanding of what companies look for in candidates, and have extensive experience in coaching and career counselling. They are also both excellent communicators. By taking you systematically through the whole career change process, Jane and Camilla's book will not only help you overcome any anxiety you may have in the face of change but provide a solid framework for taking sound career management decisions.'
Rosie Innes, Associate Director, MBA Career Services, IESE Business School

'A focus on interest, or better still passion, fascination, or enthusiasm, is crucial in career assessment and planning...and should always be the starting point, not a bolted-on afterthought. When we get this bit right, work is easy! Your book seems to address all the key issues in career self assessment and job search, in the right order. Combined with case studies which capture the "energy" of some successful career changers who have followed their passion, you provide a comprehensive and encouraging handbook for the motivated career changer.'

Clare Brachi Stott, MBA Career Development Manager, University of Bath School of Management

'This approach helped me to develop my career strategy by rediscovering motivations and interests which have remained hidden for many years. The book is interesting, readable and, most importantly, it is an excellent source of practical and realistic advice.'

Oliver Harley, NHS Plastic Surgery Specialist Registrar

'An essential read for anyone looking to better understand their personal and career aspirations, and achieve an optimal work/life balance. Self knowledge is a critical premise to attaining fulfilment and success. The book is packed with insights, practical step by step tools and examples to help facilitate the journey.'

Simon Tankard, Director: Executive Education, University of Pretoria

'An excellent guide for personal career advancement, well structured with a very practical approach that is hard to come across. An invaluable read for anyone who wants to make more out of their career.'

Thanos Mytilinaios, HR Director at Euroclinic Group

'It is a sad fact that only a minority of people follow a vocation and find happiness in their careers. Jane and Camilla's book takes the career-change crossroad as a starting point and offers practical, researched advice for taking a new career path. It is an excellent handbook for all those who are uncomfortable in their current job but are afraid or uninformed of how to make a change.'

Jerry Gray, Managing Director, Alcedo and former Chief Operating Officer, Korn Ferry International UK

If Not Now, When?

If Not Now, When?

How to Take Charge of Your Career

Camilla Arnold and Jane Barrett

BLOOMSBURY
LONDON • NEW DELHI • NEW YORK • SYDNEY

First published in Great Britain 2010

Bloomsbury Publishing
London, New Delhi, New York and Sydney
50 Bedford Square, London WC1B 3DP
www.bloomsbury.com

A CIP record for this book is available from the British Library.

ISBN: 9-781-4081-2505-2

10 9 8 7 6 5 4 3 2

Design by Fiona Pike, Pike Design, Winchester
Typeset by Saxon Graphics Ltd, Derby
Printed and bound in Great Britain by CPI Group (UK) Ltd,
Croydon CR0 4YY

CONTENTS

ACKNOWLEDGEMENTS

To my husband Colin and son Tom for bearing with me while I wrote this book. Jane

Thank you to my family for their love, support and encouragement. Camilla

Thank you to everyone who has contributed their story to the book, showing just what is possible with drive, enthusiasm and motivation. We would also like to thank all our clients over the years who have helped develop this methodology with their successes and their feedback.

INTRODUCTION

We wanted to write a book that *we* would have wanted to read when each of us was going through our own career reviews and then later as career coaches; a book we would want to use to support our clients. It's true there are many career books on the market but we feel there are none that cover the whole process from deciding what you have to offer and what you want, right through to the practicalities of securing the work you want to do, with real-life case studies to encourage you along the way. Most people don't have the time or inclination to read several books on this important topic, so we decided to put everything in one place and look at all the main areas that our clients ask us to cover with them.

This book is based on over 20 years' experience of managing careers, both our own and those of the clients we have worked with. It also draws on our experience of recruitment both in-house and for executive recruitment companies, as well as working in the field of career development with many different people from tree surgeons to venture capitalists, school leavers to recent retirees. We have created a book that reflects everything we have learnt and sets out a clear, simple structure with tips and techniques to help you analyse and plan the next step of your career.

Throughout the book there are examples of people who have successfully found work that is satisfying, meaningful and that 'fits' them. Career management is not an exact science and consequently many people haven't a clue where to start – a feeling we have known only too well! In our experience many people who are unhappy in their current role, or are unsure about how to develop their career, want to take control rather than let their career just 'happen' but they're just not sure how to get started.

IT'S UP TO YOU

What we do to earn money takes up a huge proportion of our time and affects many areas of our life, so it makes sense to devote time and energy to actively working on it and to make it as enjoyable as possible. Having said that, most people will spend more time and effort deciding on their next holiday, gadget or clothes purchase! Over the past 25 years, career management has changed immeasurably. Once it was the responsibility of the company you joined straight from school or university to guide your career as you progressed up the totem pole, with employees rarely changing career or even company. Today, it is falling to the individual to manage their career, deciding where they want to go, how to get there and which organisation or part of an organisation would be the best place to get that experience.

As a career can have such a huge impact on both everyday and long-term happiness, we encourage you to do everything you can to ensure you are in the right place, doing something that aligns with what you value and is helping you progress to your ultimate goal. For many of us the right field of work in our twenties might not reflect the person we are later on in our lives. Sometimes a review is enforced by redundancy or you may find yourself wanting to change aspects of your career as your life circumstances change. This book will help you assess your choices so you have a personal framework in which to analyse your career options.

REALITY CHECK

One caveat at this point – many people say that they'll know they have found the right career for them if they bounce out of bed in the morning, eager to get to work. The reality is that if you find your perfect job, this may not happen every day. We will aim to keep your feet on the ground as you work your way through the book; we have seen so many people find the right career at the right time for them that we believe you can do the same.

It can take time to move towards a job you'll love and time to structure your work to better suit who you are but the rewards, if you stick with it, are immeasurable. Your career also needs regular review (ideally annually) as you or your circumstances change.

By structuring your thinking using the exercises in this book, you can save time and gain more satisfaction from working towards your goal. It is apparent that in times of either boom or bust, no one manages your career better than you, as only you know what is right for you. It makes sense that people increasingly want to manage their career more proactively to get the best return for the money spent on education and the many hours they put in at work, not just leaving it to chance. That is where this book comes in.

WHY DID WE WRITE THIS BOOK?

Through our workshops and one-to-one work, we have coached thousands of people through this methodology to find successful, fulfilling careers and new roles. We have also both changed our own careers so know at first hand the anxieties, obstacles and finally relief and pleasure of finding the right career path both in the short and long-term.

JANE CASE STUDY

Originally I trained as a chartered surveyor following a suggestion by my school careers adviser to do a more vocational degree rather than geography, my best subject. I found I was interested more in people than buildings and embarked on a quest to work out what I really wanted to do. This was more difficult than I imagined – the government-run guidance offices didn't seem to offer much advice on finding work that suited me and my university careers centre was more geared towards recent students graduating. After my surveying exams, I moved to a recruitment firm thinking, naively, it was about 'helping people find work'. Blinded by the money (my values around this time were very money oriented as I had student loans to pay back!) I joined the IT recruitment division. With too much emphasis on sales, after two years I moved up the value chain and joined a headhunting company. With a less overt sales-oriented culture, I found satisfaction in delivering a more professional service but I found I enjoyed the candidate-facing work the most, which was not what I was being paid to do!

At this point I was unfulfilled but having made some career mistakes in the past (or that was how I saw them) I was reluctant to make a change and was stuck in inertia. On holiday I read an article on career coaching and on my return hired a coach to help me work out my next step. She used insightful questioning to help me discover what was important to me, what I had to offer and what motivated me.

Then I began the path to setting up my own career coaching and information company, Workmaze Ltd. I made a gradual transition, easing into this with some part-time recruitment contracts to allow me to gain more knowledge about what employers were looking for and to give me time to retrain as a career coach. I started to build relationships with business schools who could give me a steady stream of clients to support my practice.

Now Workmaze delivers career coaching and information to leading business schools world wide and I work with all types of clients from school leavers, graduates, professionals, business owners and managing directors from all over the world. There have been some blind alleys on the way, including setting up an eco-products business (environment is a strong value for me). This ultimately failed as I was too late to the market and I wasn't prepared to invest the time and money required. It was a false start but one which I learned so much from. I am now involved in eco groups at a local school and my local church which honours my interest and values in this area.

Having been involved in careers and recruitment for over 10 years, I strongly believe active career management is crucial to a successful career. The world of work changes rapidly and if you are not actively managing your career you can feel out of control and at the mercy of circumstances. I hope this book is something clients can come back to when things are out of kilter and use it as a structure to analyse and make plans to develop their careers.

CAMILLA CASE STUDY

My career started like that of most of my friends and early colleagues; we fell into jobs that seemed to be as good as any other at the time and had some scope for progression. It was a rarity to come across someone who absolutely knew what they wanted to do and had made choices from A levels and university onwards towards that goal. To be honest, most of us looked at these strange creatures with a mixture of awe and envy wondering why we couldn't work out what was the right direction for us. The perennial advice then, as now, was to work out what you were interested in and then find a career from that. The only problem with that was that I really didn't think that there was anything in particular that interested me enough to 'put all my eggs in that basket' – socialising and travel didn't really seem to offer many long-term career options.

I have been hugely fortunate in the different jobs I have held; I have enjoyed each and every one and learned from them all, so I felt I was progressing. The only problem was that it just felt like a series of jobs that I fell into through referral or happy circumstance rather than a career per se. Each time I thought I was ready for a new direction I would buy the latest book on how to identify your passion and find that I was still fairly clueless as to what the next steps would be. Instead, I listened to what other colleagues and friends said were my strengths and oriented my career around them, namely my ability to organise effectively and problem solve. As a result I had an eclectic career based upon those perceived strengths and was always hopeful I would stumble across the perfect job for me but I don't think I ever quite believed it would happen.

After 20 years of working, I finally did exactly that – I stumbled across coaching (a form of problem solving) and the concept of a portfolio career which would allow me to have the variety that I loved. I spent three years transitioning from my previous role as Operations Director for a leading headhunting firm to my current career and I finally feel I have found the right road for me. It would not suit everyone but it harnesses all my strengths, my preferences for working environment and rewards, whilst still offering new challenges as I constantly refine my career path as I develop and identify new aspirations. At each stage of this career transition, I have revised and reviewed where I am and whether it works for me. I tried coaching full-time and found I missed the buzz of the office and interaction with colleagues so I re-evaluated and after much searching, eventually found a company focused on coaching and talent development – TXG Ltd. The company's values and drive to be the best in the business matched mine exactly. I am now TXG's global Head of Coaching and advise blue chip corporate clients on executive coaching whilst acting as a broker for the best coaching talent worldwide. I also maintain my own coaching practice, Total Clarity, which allows me the flexibility I was searching for and allows me to express all aspects of who I am in the work place. I coach a wide range of clients from CEOs, board directors and career professionals who are looking to work to their best potential through to those seeking their perfect career but are not sure where to start, ranging from recent graduates to retirees.

For both of us looking back, if we had known then what we know now (how many times do people say that?!), we both agree we could probably have shortened the whole process and had a clearer idea of where we were going. Our journeys from job to chosen career have been long ones. We spent years searching for the right careers and we became frustrated at the lack of informed practical advice to get moving. The books we read tended to skim over the top of the subject and while we ended up with a glut of information, we received little practical advice on how to decide on a career option. Advice from well-intentioned advisers was that if you had a good job, why rock the boat? That is why we now work with the clients looking for help with their career search and why we have decided to write this book. We hope that it provides you with a structure based on years of experience that is clear, easy to follow, pragmatic and takes you beyond a download of information to how to follow through to your ultimate goal of a great career that you manage proactively. We truly believe it is possible for anyone to do the same if they have the motivation and drive to keep going, even when the going gets tough. It should also be a fun exploration of you and your personal brand.

WHAT THIS BOOK WILL GIVE YOU:

- A structured series of exercises which focus on each specific element of career planning
- Clarity about what is **really** important to you in your working life and what is a 'nice to have'
- Insights from other people who have been through a career change and successfully come out the other side
- A reference book you can return to again and again throughout your career that covers the key aspects of career planning and change
- A proven system that works. We keep in touch with our clients to ensure that these exercises and our advice is still helpful and relevant across sectors, industries and geographies
- A way to investigate career options in a logical and structured way
- An action plan and timetable to move forward backed up by solid analysis

Often people start thinking about their career when a crisis hits: they have been made redundant, had a low salary review or been passed over for promotion. In an ideal world, this kind of outside influence should not be the catalyst to thinking about your career, as the emotion attached to it can cloud your thinking and a new job search starts from a position of hurt, anger and resentment rather than enthusiasm, drive and commitment. For many of our clients, however, we often work on the 'I need to get a job now' issues (CVs, job search strategy, getting interviews etc.) in parallel with the longer term 'I want to find a job that fits me better' ambitions.

Career choices can seem confusing and overwhelming at times but it can be reassuring to work through a proven process in order to analyse your career. Once you have completed the book, you will have a much better understanding of what you want and what you have to offer. The career framework you will have created by the end of the book will be a summary of your personal data collected in a methodical way. This will allow you to make an informed choice, minimising the chance that you will make the wrong decision.

HOW TO USE THE BOOK:

Our experience has shown that what you get out of the process and the clarity you have at the end of the process depends entirely on how much you put into it. It can be tempting just to read through a book like this, vowing to get back to the exercises at a later date. Unfortunately, this approach is not going to lead to any lasting changes. We strongly encourage you to complete all the exercises as you come across them. If you would like soft copies of the exercises, you will find them at our website **www.howtotakechargeofyourcareer.com** along with other resources that may be useful. Keep an action planning sheet to create momentum and a timeline for completing the various tasks, all of which we'll cover later. You will then start to reap the rewards of your hard work.

Many people will be able to complete the exercises and will have the motivation to set them on the path to proactively managing their career. However, some may find this challenging and may wish to work with a career coach. There are many career coaches on the market, some good, some not so good. Later in the book, we will give you some insider knowledge of how to choose the right one for you.

WHO IS THIS BOOK FOR?

Whether you are looking for a new job or seeking a promotion, planning to change career or set up your own business, this book has been written for you so that you get the most satisfaction out of your work.

Our experience has shown that the knowledge you will gain from the book will give you an advantage if you are:

Looking for a new job – as a candidate, if you know what you want and what you can offer, you will be more compelling as a potential employee than those who haven't worked that out.

Looking to be promoted or progress within an organisation – if you know clearly what skills you have, what you want to develop and where you are heading in terms of your career, you are far more likely to achieve your goals.

Finding the right career direction – if you are clear about what you are looking for, what skills you bring and you have done the research to confirm your career choice, you will have a clear direction when starting your job search.

Setting up a new business – ensuring that setting up a business serves your personal needs, values and skills is the key to success and may also help you when you hire staff to complement your skills.

Post retirement – analysing your working life to date, the skills you have accumulated and the preferences you have for considering working will help in finding a role to suit you if you decide to keep working.

Embarking upon education – if you have identified your long-term aims for your career, you are more likely to make sure you are on the right course and, once you are on that course, ensure you maximise the opportunities that it provides.

IN SUMMARY

Many of the articles and books that have been written on this subject will target only one particular aspect of the search for the ideal career whether it is identifying your passion, understanding portfolio working, creating the perfect CV or answering the most dastardly of interview questions. Many of these books may be useful to you and we recommend the best in the 'Resources' section at the back of the book. By covering all the key aspects of a career search and ongoing career planning in one book, we believe you can complete the fundamental groundwork to really know yourself, what you are looking for and understand all the steps to get there. There are no guarantees in life but our tried and tested methodology will lead you to making an informed decision, based on skill identification and research to create an action plan to get you where you want to go.

If there is a particular stage that you are tempted to miss out, it is probably the stage that will hold the key to the direction for you to take. We will encourage you to network (which usually makes people's spirits falter at the mere mention of the word) but we will also give you tips about how to make the process as painless as possible. Sadly there is no getting around networking – it has huge value not only in identifying your next career or the next role but also in developing your long-term career. It is easy to sit back and just go with the flow, avoiding the more difficult aspects of striving for a great career rather than just allowing life to happen to us. We encourage you to become proactive because the rewards really are worth it.

We all have choices in life but if you have ever contemplated a career change, or tried to identify a career path that excites you, we ask the question – if not now, when?

PART ONE: IF NOT NOW, WHEN? WHAT'S HOLDING YOU BACK?

'Whether you think you can or you can't, you're right.'

HENRY FORD, founder of the Ford Motor Company

Dealing with obstacles may seem an unusual place to start in a book about seizing the moment and making a change in your career but when we speak to a client for the first time, often the first thing they want to talk about is all the problems that might get in the way of their success.

Those areas of concern include:

- lack of motivation;
- limiting beliefs about their ability to find something that works for them;
- frustration and anger if a career change has been forced on them (i.e. through redundancy, illness or another life-changing circumstance);
- lack of time;
- lack of money or unwillingness to take a drop in salary or retrain;
- family and/or friends questioning why they are considering a change.

We have covered each of these areas of concern below to give you some ideas as to how you might overcome them and how others who have faced similar concerns have found a way to move forward. If you find that any of these, or indeed other concerns, are slowing you down or stopping you from realising your potential, you may want to consider finding a coach or therapist to help you deal with them once and for all.

1. Overcoming fear and risk

'The greatest hazard in life is to risk nothing.'
STEVE JOBS, co-founder of Apple Inc.

Fear can be paralysing but knowing and understanding what your fear is can be the first step towards facing it. The best antidote to fear when going through a career change we have found is to work out whether your fear is based in reality or is merely a perception. So, it is reality that you can't become a brain surgeon without having trained as a doctor but it is perception that they don't accept people over 25 on to courses to train as doctors.

By naming the fear, you can then gather as much evidence and facts to deal with what is real and what is assumed and dismiss the negative perceptions that are holding you back.

Many people seem to feel that if they do nothing, that it will all work out eventually and they will deal with bumps in the road as they come along. They will do almost anything not to make a choice to move forward. The irony is that deciding to do nothing is also a choice and often means that people are at the whim of factors outside their control.

Calculated risk

There's no getting around it, at some point, if you are going to move forward, you will have to take a leap of faith but by basing it on research and knowledge, it **will** feel less daunting. There's a moment in *Indiana Jones and the Last Crusade* when Indiana is faced with a seemingly insurmountable chasm to cross to get to the Holy Grail. He knows his subject and his journey up to that point has been reliant on his knowledge to avoid the pitfalls put in his way. At the chasm, however, he has to trust his instincts and steps out into the seeming abyss to find a hidden bridge. What would it take for you to take that leap of faith in your search for your career?

If you are getting stuck, it can be useful to highlight the sticking points and come up with an action plan to solve them:

PROBLEM/STICKING POINT	RESOLUTION OPTIONS
e.g. I won't make enough money for at least two years to support our current lifestyle.	e.g. Review current lifestyle and see where there are potential savings we could live with for two years.
	Build up a savings account to cover the difference between the new salary and the amount needed to support our lifestyle.
	Take out a career development loan for the retraining and use savings for extra living expenses over the next two years.

	Investigate home swapping instead of normal family holiday.
	Apply for a mortgage holiday for two years.

2. Finding the right motivation and attitude

'Attitude is a little thing that makes a big difference.'
WINSTON CHURCHILL,
British statesman and Prime Minister during World War II

If there is one thing that we have found over and over again as we work with people going through the process of deciding on a career direction or career change, it's that the people who are successful are motivated and have the right positive attitude. The people who get to the end of the exercises and research knowing their future career direction are the ones who have soldiered on past obstacles, scepticism, nerves, lack of confidence and time constraints. We know from experience that this is often easier said than done but we hope this section will help you when you come across some of the hurdles that will surely occur as you work your way through the book.

Finding your motivation

It is so important you find the motivation within yourself to make the change. Just flicking through this book hoping that change will happen by osmosis is sadly not going to work, as only you can put in the effort to make it happen. It also rarely works well if you are pushing someone to make a career change and working your way through the book for them (perhaps you're a well-meaning parent or partner).

Once you have found your motivation, it's important to maintain your positive attitude, even when the chips are down. We hope we can help you achieve that attitude by providing case studies of people who have been down this road before you and have been successful.

Sometimes when you are struggling, this means having to 'fake it 'til you make it' – faking the confidence and self belief until things start to fall into place. It is surprising how effective this can be as a strategy to keep the momentum going and move through your doubts. There has been plenty of research and even television shows that have taken people out of their comfort zone and taught them how to fake a situation until they had achieved the insider language, the confidence and the basic skills to make people believe in them and their abilities.

The faking can be tough to start off with, whether it is convincing people you are confident and positive about the career you have decided upon or overcoming nerves to go along to an information gathering interview. We have seen time and time again that there is a point where you move from being a faker to the person who has made it and it starts to become second nature. You can use the same strategies as we go through this methodology together – it is amazing how effective it can be, especially if you are feeling a little sceptical or lacking in confidence. Once you have some experience, even if it is unpaid or for a relatively short period of time, often it can be 'enough' to help you to come across as knowledgeable in that area.

As a relatively new consultant following his career change, James was only ever asked about what he could do for his clients and what examples he had of recent successes. He was never asked how long he had been consulting, which definitely helped when he was first starting out. James had learnt to be confident in a new area where he had limited experience although what little he did have was extremely relevant. He never volunteered the information about how little experience he had and he chose to focus on what he *could* do.

All change is risky and as human beings many of us will do almost anything to avoid change until we have no way around it. While you can't remove all the risk when it comes to progressing or changing your career, sometimes staying where you are may actually be the more risky option and much less satisfying in the long term. For some, it can take years to transition to a new career, retrain or progress within an organisation and so change can be a gradual process where you can test the water rather than having to commit too much too soon.

Attitude to change exercise

If you do find your resolve wobbling and feel that perhaps this is just all too much trouble, it's worth considering the following questions:

If you do nothing at all where might you be in five years' time?

How do you feel about this answer?

What is the risk to you of not making a change?

What is the block that is getting in your way?

If that block was no longer an issue, what would you do next?

We encourage you to keep going even if you realise that your career change or progression is going to take longer than you envisioned. The end result will be worth it and you are not alone – many of our clients have faced the same concern but were so pleased that they kept going. You may also find that once you have decided on your career move, you get blown off course by an unexpected event or change in circumstances, however, if you keep the momentum, drive and attitude, if you know where you are heading then you are much more likely to reach your destination.

HENRY TEARE — CASE STUDY

Having gone to university and completed a business degree, I still wasn't sure what I wanted to do for a career. A lot of friends were going into banking and I thought I should do the same, as it seemed like a good idea to pay off some debts. I soon realised that I didn't want to be a small cog in a large machine and fell into selling advertising space for a small firm instead. Still unfulfilled, I finally realised, having always known it deep down, that I dreamed of doing something creative with my hands, away from an office environment.

Disappointed in the haircuts I had been getting, I started cutting my own hair and then friends started asking to have theirs done too. At that stage, I was looking at getting into carpentry, landscape gardening or building and hadn't really thought about hairdressing as an option. Then one night, I awoke in a panic, worried about a presentation to a media agency I hadn't really prepared for and it clicked. I couldn't carry on like this. I had to be happy, passionate and proud of my work. I started thinking about which profession was going to suit me the most and the more I thought about hairdressing the more it ticked the right lifestyle choices. I'd be creative and active in my work, gain a skill with the potential to travel and most importantly make people happy every day.

I set about meeting hairdressers and getting work experience in the evening and at the weekend. The more I did it, the more I wanted to learn and then I met a former Vidal Sassoon Educator, who was setting up a salon and I jumped at the opportunity to join him. I knew it was going to be tough financially and that I had to train from the bottom again, but I had to give it a go.

It took a couple of years of hard work but once I realised I was an able hairdresser, I finally became proud of my achievements for the first time since I was a teenager. I am now five years into my hairdressing career and recently got a job at a top salon, James Brown, in the West End of London. Those early days of worrying about failing are all in the past and I am looking forward to opening new doors in hairdressing.

> What helped me initially was to imagine myself in the same job in five to ten years time. Did I want to be that person? Unhappy in my work and unfulfilled, stuck in a rut? I think the key is to be passionate, whether it's about a skill, service or product you sell, then take small steps towards finding out more about it. The learning will then come easily. That passion will drive success and a better quality of life will follow.

3. Limiting beliefs

'There is only one cause of unhappiness: the false beliefs you have in your head, beliefs so widespread, so commonly held, that it never occurs to you to question them.'
ANTHONY DE MELLO, spiritual guide, writer and speaker

One thing is certain as you go through this process. You will face obstacles along the way, both real and imagined, and whether you get past them or get stuck comes down largely to attitude.

Often the most powerful hurdles we face are the imagined ones. If you have ever had coaching or read anything about the subject, you may have heard these described as self-limiting beliefs. These are the beliefs that we have gathered through life that may, at some time, have worked well for us but we rarely examine whether they are still helpful. These beliefs often start from things we hear from an early age – common examples are things like:

'I have never been very bright.'
'It's a pipe dream to expect to find the perfect job.'
'My family has always struggled in the work place and I expect the same will be true for me.'
'My dad always joked with me that I had great plans but never achieved them.'
'I'm lucky to have a job – thinking I can find something I'll enjoy as I earn money is not reality.'
'I am never going to be a big earner.'
'I tend to drift and be a bit lazy – my teacher used to tell me that I was never going to get to the highest levels of a career.'

'I was told by my professor that I should stick to working with figures as I wasn't that great with people.'

The list could go on and on. So the first step for you at this stage is to be honest with yourself and write a list of the thoughts that are getting in your way. Do you think you'll fail? Why? The more things you uncover, the better!

Camilla recently coached someone who had been put off becoming a copywriter when she was 15 after her grandmother and farmer father had said that it didn't sound a good way to earn a living. When we discussed what they were basing that belief on, she discussed it with both of them and they couldn't remember the conversation that had stopped her career dream in its tracks. She is now studying copywriting part-time and is talking to people in the field before making the move into advertising full-time. It may seem obvious but you always have the choice about how you react to what is said to you; it is up to you how you hear what is being said. When someone offers advice or points you away from a direction you are thinking about, it is always worth asking yourself why they have given you the advice they have, what have they based that advice on and whether they see your future in the same way you do. You can then decide to take that advice or not, or just chalk it up as an opinion that is not helpful in this instance.

We find in our coaching practices that clients who spend their time with people who have achieved what they set out to achieve get the most supportive comments from them as they know anything is possible. They have been there, done that and got the t-shirt!

Identify obstacles exercise

Getting to the bottom of your limiting beliefs is really important, so that you recognise them should they start getting in your way and are hopefully able to deal with them one at a time. You will find as we continue that more of these limiting beliefs pop up either in your own head or are contributed by well-meaning friends and family. Keep going back to this first action step to validate whether it is something to bear in mind or to leave to one side.

1. List one self-limiting belief.

---

2. Who told you this?

---

3. Is their opinion based on fact or evidence or is it just an opinion? If you are not sure, ask them to give you some evidence to back up what they're saying.

---

4. Are they equipped to give you good advice on the particular subject they are commenting on?

---

5. Do you know someone else with whom you can check this advice or statement?

As you keep adding to your list of self-limiting beliefs, ask yourself if it is helping or hindering you? If you were to suspend that belief for a moment, how differently would you approach the situation? Sometimes these worries come from within. Perhaps you have had a bad day and wonder, Am I clever enough?, or I don't interview well so what's the point?, or I'll never be able to do that so I may as well not try. There are those self-limiting beliefs again. You will find that this is a bit like peeling an onion – just when you think you've got to the last layer, there's another one but the more you uncover and deal with, the fewer obstacles you are likely to face!

Jane remembers telephoning one of her oldest friends to tell her that she was moving from recruitment to be a career coach. The friend shouted to her husband while on the phone to her, saying:

'Jane says she going to be a career coach! You can't make any money doing that can you?' she then categorically told Jane they thought she would never make any money from career coaching. Several years passed and Jane set up a successful coaching business. Ironically, Jane stayed overnight with these friends before delivering a career coaching workshop at a local university which, incidentally, she got paid for!

When you are dealing with your limiting beliefs, it can be difficult to stay positive because for so many of us, the doubts and negative thoughts seem to flow so much easier. If that resonates with you, then perhaps it is worth creating a 'positives' folder.

This folder can be filled with any positive feedback you have received over the years – cards, letters of recommendation, good reports, thank you emails from managers or colleagues – you get the idea. When you start to wonder whether you have the ability, reading through some of those can help get you back to reality and remind you of your abilities with solid evidence. This file can also come in useful when you are compiling a CV to remind you of your achievements or skills.

It can also be helpful to enlist the support of a friend or perhaps a family member who will challenge some of your thinking at times. One word of warning, enlist the help of people who are supportive and challenging rather than those who are well-intentioned but seem to have an agenda of their own (i.e. does it suit them if you stay at the same level as them? Do they see you in a certain way and not want you to change? etc.).

4. I didn't choose to make a change – it's been forced on me

'When it is dark enough, you can see the stars.'
RALPH WALDO EMERSON, American philosopher and poet

Sometimes we face life-changing events that can throw us off course, even if that course wasn't right for us anyway. Nicky Hambleton-Jones was made redundant three times before she finally threw in the towel and worked out what she wanted to do with her life. This took financial reserves and risk but eventually her determination and enthusiasm for the field she had chosen took her right to the top of the image consulting profession.

How you respond after you have dealt with the immediate aftermath of any life-changing event, where something happens that is outside your control, often determines whether you are able to move forward in a constructive way. We have seen at first hand how hard this can be and we know there will be ups and downs but we have also seen that it is increasingly common for a life-changing event to send people in a new or more focused direction.

JOHN SMITH — CASE STUDY

I spent 20 years in the investment banking industry, firstly as an equity market analyst, and more latterly as a leader of various City firms. My final role was as Global Head of Equities at ABN Amro, with responsibility for 2,500 people in 45 countries and over €1bn of revenue. I spent my time flying around the world, building teams, deciding strategy and driving the business to an improved P&L.

The change for me came when our third child was diagnosed as autistic just before his fourth birthday. At that stage, Fraser was non-verbal, very difficult behaviourally and a real handful.

It was a fairly simple decision to give up work, train as a behavioural therapist and to work full-time with my son. He began to improve, and six years later – whilst still noticeably autistic – he now has lots of language, is a happy and cheerful little boy and we live a relatively normal life.

What was unexpected was how relevant the behavioural work was to my previous world in the City, most particularly around how people learn, what motivates them, and how the behaviour of leaders can influence those that follow them.

By this stage, I was also being asked to mentor younger people coming through the ranks in my old industry and it seemed an obvious step to find an outlet for this and to couple it with my behavioural work. As Fraser began to improve, I had capacity to do other things, but I still needed flexibility around his needs and deficits.

The answer lay in executive coaching. For the past five years I have built my own coaching practice and have worked with hundreds of clients on a one-to-one basis to help them improve their performance. I have worked in consultancy, accountancy, the legal profession, government, real estate, private equity and multiple investment banks. I now work around three days a week, have flexibility around when I do this and I am lucky enough to have a fulfilling, varied and interesting job – fulfillment for me comes from seeing people clear obstacles and achieve their potential.

For me, the lesson from this was to decide what was important in my life and build work around that rather than the opposite. Coupled with treating a huge challenge as a learning opportunity, I am both delighted and relieved by how it has worked out for us all.

Elisabeth Kübler-Ross first introduced the Kübler-Ross model in her 1969 book *On Death and Dying*. The model is more commonly known as the five stages of grief or change. Originally this model was used to understand the stages one might go through when facing a terminal illness but was later extended to cover other severe personal losses such as a job loss or major change. It's still a useful model for those clients who get stuck at a certain stage so they can see where they are and understand it is a perfectly normal response that they will work their way through.

Stage 1 – Denial

- **'I am not at risk, this isn't happening to me', 'I am too good for this to happen to me.'**

Stage 2 – Anger

- 'How dare they make me redundant', 'After all the years of service, this is how they treat me.'

Stage 3 – Bargaining

- 'Perhaps if I reduce my hours', 'What if I offer to reduce my pay?'

Stage 4 – Depression

- 'I am on the scrapheap', 'I'll never get another job as good as this.'

Stage 5 – Acceptance

- 'It is up to me, so I might as well get on with it', 'Well I might as well look on the bright side.'

If you have picked up this book as a result of a life-changing event but are struggling with how to move forward, you might want to consider working with a therapist or coach to help you establish what is getting in your way, whether you are ready to start moving forward and how you are going to do that.

As we said at the beginning of this section, as with so many things in life, it is all down to your attitude and if and how you decide to go forward.

CLAUDIA BERMUDEZ CASE STUDY

I was laid off in June 2008. Although I was sad to lose my job, I soon realised it was a blessing in disguise; being out of work gave me the time I needed to re-evaluate my life and I knew that I didn't want to continue with my current career. After working in the charitable sector for 14 years I knew I wanted to change my career. I was tired of working long hours in an office.

A colleague of mine had taught English in South Korea and suggested that I should try it – I was already contemplating doing something with languages. I decided to give it a try, went through the application process and organised my work visa. Next, after much consideration, I sold my worldly possessions and booked a flight to South Korea. It was exciting and scary. I felt like I was jumping into the unknown.

> I have been working in South Korea for four months now. I am teaching English to grade school and high school students. I love teaching English – it's wonderful to see your students' progress. Coming to South Korea has given me a new lease of life; it's also taught me to be more flexible and to adjust to different situations such as the language and culture in another country. You also have to adjust to a new work culture. Working in South Korea will give me the necessary experience I need to embark on a new career in teaching.
>
> When I finish working in South Korea I plan to pursue a Master's degree in teaching in the US or UK.

5. Finding the time and momentum to make it happen

'Do not wait; the time will never be "just right". Start where you stand and work with whatever tools you may have at your command and better tools will be found as you go along.'
NAPOLEON HILL, American motivational writer on wealth

One of the main perceived obstacles to working on your career is lack of time. We regularly hear that this is an obstacle when we start working with clients and we have to admit that we have used this excuse many times ourselves.

If you do think this will be a problem, it is worth asking yourself if you are sufficiently excited about your goals to commit the time to working towards them. Is there anything you can do to motivate yourself? Can you break down your career change or shift to smaller, more distinct goals so it feels more manageable?

Our experience is that if you set yourself achievable goals that fire you up, you are more likely to prioritise your time and when you analyse how you spend your days, perhaps you can see how you can carve out extra time. Perhaps it means watching less TV or getting up half an hour earlier. If you are sufficiently motivated you will find a creative way to make the time to work on your career.

While this is not a book on time management (and we recommend one in the References section if you are struggling with the subject), being effective with the time you have to devote to your career will pay dividends.

Having a realistic time frame to change your career is also important as many clients seem to lose their enthusiasm and momentum if they let the whole process drift. You may want to work with a friend or partner who is also interested in doing a career review to keep each other going throughout the process when one of you starts to flag.

6. The money question

'Old men are always advising young men to save money. That is bad advice. Don't save every nickel. Invest in yourself. I never saved a dollar until I was forty years old.'
HENRY FORD, Founder of the Ford Motor Company

Money…the biggie and the next major hurdle that holds people back from really going after what they want in their career. Common worries include, 'Will I have to take a salary cut to retrain?' 'How will I adapt to a reduced cash flow?' 'How will I cope with the financial uncertainty?' There is no getting around this subject for most people and it really can't be ignored in the hope it will go away (a technique we have seen many people try over the years). It is important that you look at the issue, research your options and make a plan so you feel as secure as you can be at every step.

When Camilla talks to a potential client, she often likens changing career to deciding to train as a trapeze artist. The client usually approaches the whole thing with a sense of slight excitement but also with an element of fear that they will fail or it won't be possible. They imagine showing up at the big top to learn how to become a trapeze artist and being asked immediately to don the Lycra, climb 30 ft in the air, swing on the trapeze and leap as the dashing young man comes swinging towards them with arms outstretched. They seem to feel the same way about approaching a career change – all a bit scary, exhilarating if it works and downright painful if it all goes wrong. No wonder they are daunted. In actuality, the trainer at the big top is there to help you through the learning process with as little pain as possible and preferably without the Lycra! You would be fitted with a tight safety harness to protect you and you would start swinging on the trapeze only a few feet above the ground over a safety net. Our job as coach in this scenario is to define what your safety net and safety harness look like; very often it is money and having a financial cushion to give protection. Once the safety net and harness are in place, there is a point in this process when the client wants to climb higher, is ready to take off the safety harness and then feels that they are so comfortable on the first trapeze that they are ready to take the leap of faith and be caught by the person on the other trapeze. So, in this analogy – what would your safety harness and safety net look like? Would having enough money to make the change be one of them?

As you go through the book, there will be a point when you have an idea of what you want to do and an action plan of how you are going to achieve it – then the money hurdle may well appear. It may cost you money, either lost income in terms of a change in salary or the necessity to pay for training etc. But before you worry that the money hurdle is going to stop you in your tracks, here are just a few things you might want to consider:

- Get real and work out what money you are going to need in your financial safety net or piggy bank to make this happen.
- Devise a specific action plan on how you are going to make that happen.
- Draw up a budget of your monthly expenditure, going through each item to see if there is any room for saving and cutting back.
- Are you going to need a period of time to start saving for the financial safety net?
- Are you going to see if there is a loan available?
- Might you be able to work part time while you retrain?
- Check again – how much money are you really going to need for a finite amount of time while you make the move and how long can you survive on reduced means?

If money is an issue for you, only you know how much you are going to need to survive while you make these changes and reduce your stress. Be realistic. If it takes you a little longer to achieve your goal while you create your financial safety net, it is time well spent as long as you maintain your momentum and find things to do in parallel that advance your career aspirations with further networking, research etc.

Be aware that some careers will require you to find money for retraining and equipment and this obviously needs to be factored into your overall plan. Sometimes it is surprising just how much facilities or equipment cost; this is something to find out in the research phase of your career process.

Undoubtedly there are commitments that sometimes are absolutely key (child support payments, mortgage or rent) but even seemingly immoveable commitments might not be as inflexible as you think: we have had clients who have taken their children out of private schools to move to an area where there are good state schools, and some who have downsized to a smaller property or relocated to another part of the country where the properties are more affordable, in order to release some money to enable a change of career to take place.

COLIN BARRETT CASE STUDY

In October 1993 I graduated from university with a 2:1 in philosophy and no idea about what to do with my life. I'd dipped my toe in the water of the university careers centre without much success (apparently only the Roman Catholic Church was interested in employing philosophy graduates), so I started replying to pretty much any advert for a 'graduate' job that appeared in the press.

My first job was with a large life assurance company in Kent. From there I moved to Lloyd's of London, and then on to Reuters. There was no great plan, just a desire to be in London and work for a household name. I fell into a job called product management, which involves a small amount of technical knowledge, large amounts of common sense and an ability to be vaguely organised.

I did my time in the big corporate, travelled a bit, went out a lot and generally had a good time. However, towards the end of the nineties it became pretty clear to me that I wasn't on anyone's radar to be fast-tracked through the ranks; I worked in a huge, sprawling company with a comparatively flat management structure. I got paid well, was competent at my job but my heart wasn't really in it and for that reason I think there were a lot of people ahead of me in the queue to move into the heady world of middle management.

About this time I also started to look around at colleagues who were 10–15 years older than me. These people were relatively well paid and in their early to mid forties, and most were deeply cynical about 'work'. As a group they seemed to share two things in common; their company pensions were the main reason they stayed in the job, and they were all petrified of being made redundant at the next internal reorganisation (at one point almost a fortnightly event at Reuters).

I realised two important things: one, no one was going to pluck me from obscurity and mentor me through the ranks; two, I never ever wanted to be in a position where I wasn't confident about being in charge of my own destiny.

For me the change needed to be radical. I knew I had to start again from scratch. It wasn't easy to acknowledge to myself that the first decade of my working life had been pretty much a waste of time. I had friends who were doing well and advancing professionally and here was I about to go back to square one. To do this I knew I needed to leave London, and I knew I had to find something which was going to tick all the boxes for me. Fortunately I was (and still am) lucky enough to be married to an amazing career coach who patiently helped me to identify that role.

When all the plans had finally been laid, we moved from London to Yorkshire, and I started to train for my new career as a financial planner. One of the things I realised very early on was that this was going to be a major financial undertaking. Unless we could bankroll ourselves for at least 18 months there would just be too much financial pressure and I'd probably end up going back to a product management job based up north. We needed to buy ourselves time, and that involved setting aside a large amount of money. We did this by selling our house in London and, instead of trading up, bought an equivalent sized house in Yorkshire. The price difference allowed us to bank enough money to support us during the early years of my career change.

I started my financial services career right at the bottom, learning the job from the ground up. But this time, because I had a definite plan and real drive to succeed, I rapidly progressed to the point where I was able to advise clients. Financial advice is a career where you can differentiate yourself through qualifications and so I spent two solid years taking exams (fitted in around work and a young family) to accelerate my progress.

I now own a share in a high end financial planning business, advising clients around the country. I'm not going to pretend it has always been a bed of roses – one thing I quickly found is that a company of 20 people can have just the same communication issues as a company of 20,000! But I am immeasurably happier, and I can honestly say that since making the change I have never gone into work with that 'what the hell am I doing with my life?' question floating around my head – something that was all too common when I was in London.

It has taken a long time, but now, seven years later, I am earning just about what I earned before I changed careers. In my plan I expected it to take five years for me to achieve this, but I hadn't banked on setting up a new company during that period. The difference is that now I have tremendous potential to earn much more, on my own terms, in a company that I part-own. I dread to think where I'd be now if I was still working in product management – certainly a prime candidate for a mid-life crisis.

If I could give potential career changers any useful advice it would be this: if you're thinking of making a radical change, do not underestimate how long it will take you to re-establish yourself and make sure that you have enough of a financial cushion to see it through. There will be pressure enough without financial worries to blow you off course.

For me and my family changing career involved a lot of effort, commitment and faith – but oh my goodness it was worth it.

Other options that you might consider include:

(a) Transition gradually using your existing skills

Sometimes it is possible to use your old skills to help you transition into a new field or support you in a field that doesn't pay much but that you love. Many of our clients have combined different jobs to make a portfolio career (see Chapter 23 in Part Three) where each job has a specific purpose and adds different things to their lives.

Alison originally worked as a buyer for a telecommunications company. She became interested in nutrition after reading a book on the subject and enrolled on a part-time, two year course at the Institute for Optimum Nutrition. She then started a professional practice at home while she continued her job.

After five years she started to work at a leading complementary medicine clinic in the evenings. A year later she took voluntary redundancy from her day job and she now concentrates on her work as a nutritionist.

By her own admission, Alison says that one of the disadvantages of her work is her inconsistent income, but she is willing to put up with this as she enjoys being her own boss and gets huge satisfaction from helping people improve their health and wellbeing.

She is now investigating work within schools and healthcare centres to provide another more constant stream of income to complement the fluctuating income from her private practice.

(b) Reduce your outgoings

Sometimes, if you are at a stage in your life when you are supporting just yourself, you can make the conscious choice to reduce your expenditure each month.

Kate wasn't sure what she wanted to do when she graduated with a degree in history, but when she was offered a role as a business analyst with a leading consultancy, it seemed like too good an opportunity to pass up. It was a job that was the envy of her friends, intellectually stimulating with increasing responsibility, but the 16-hour days and weekend working coupled with the patriarchal culture started to take their toll.

After nearly two years and much soul searching, she decided the job wasn't for her. She had always found that writing came easily to her and she had long been fascinated by the world of journalism, especially as several members of her family were in the field. She wanted to check whether this was a pipe dream or a reality so she wrote to several publications asking for work experience. She obtained a work experience placement on a publication and, following recognition of her enthusiasm and natural ability, was offered the chance to do a journalism course.

The money was substantially less than she had earned before but the opportunity was too good to miss. She took the course and later got a permanent job with the publication.

She still works long hours but she is now doing something that she believes in and is so much happier. She is now building a long-term career plan on how she can use her writing and background in journalism in new ways.

Kate's tip to other people looking to make a change in their careers is to take the plunge. You may have to be creative in making some changes to make it work but the upside is well worth it.

(c) Release assets or ask for financial help

Sometimes it may be an option to borrow from friends and family, your bank or to use your savings or sell assets to release enough money to achieve your goal.

John had to leave school at 18 and start earning as there wasn't the money for him to go to university. He found a series of sales jobs that came relatively easily to him and he had a lifestyle that worked for him. He bought his first car, then a flat and was regularly out with his friends. Life was fine but he knew that it really wasn't enough.

If he had been able to go to university, he would have liked to have gone into law. He decided to test out whether he was really interested in the subject and took an evening course to get his law A level. He passed with flying colours and decided that it was a case of now or never.

He sold his flat, his car and persuaded his parents to let him move back in with them while he studied for his law degree and then Articles. Many people tried to talk him out of making such a major change but he was determined to at least try. He loved the course and when it came to interviewing with major law firms, he found that his previous experience gave him a high level of confidence and an advantage over his fellow students.

He has now been working in law for six years and has never been happier.

As we have said before, when you truly know what you want (i.e. your goals) then you can make it happen if you are motivated, think creatively and have patience. Only you know what you are able and prepared to do to overcome financial hurdles but it is possible.

7. Finding support

'Keep away from those who try to belittle your ambitions. Small people always do that, but the really great make you believe that you too can become great.'

MARK TWAIN, American writer

If you are someone who naturally works away at a project without needing any support or assistance, you can fast forward to the next section. If, however, you are someone who likes input from others, seeks reassurance from family and friends when you are making big decisions or prefers working in a team rather than on your own, this is for you.

The first thing to consider is what kind of support will work for you.

- Do you like someone to challenge you?
- Do you want someone to be unconditionally on your side and act as a cheerleader as you meet your goals?
- Is there room for both challenger and cheerleader?
- During which phases of the process do you think you are most likely to need support?

Some of our clients have baulked at asking their friends for help but even superheroes have help and support: Superman had Lois Lane, Batman had Robin… Look around at the people you know and decide who might be able to offer you the type of support you are looking for. We suggest you look for people you trust to be honest with you who will give you feedback and with whom you can brainstorm ideas. It's important that they encourage you when you get stuck or feel down (sadly this is likely to happen every so often but it does pass) and can keep you to your time frame.

Having said that, remember that they will be giving subjective advice. While it is always good to gather additional support, look at it and decide whether it is useful to you or whether you feel that it is not useful to you right now – at the end of the day, it is the superhero who makes the ultimate decision.

It is also important that you let your supporters know what works for you and what you would prefer them to do more of if it is working and less of if you think it might hinder your progress.

One word of warning: other people, even people who are closest to you, may have a vested interest in keeping you just where you are. Well-meaning friends may say things like 'You're just lucky to have a good job' or 'Nobody enjoys their work'. Meaning well doesn't make the comments any more positive. You will need energy and your self esteem intact to progress in your career. So-called 'vampire friends' have to be managed carefully so that you don't get dragged down by them. If you don't think that certain friends are going to be positive influences as you look at your career, perhaps it might be a good idea not to dwell on the subject when you meet with them or solicit their advice at least while you are going through this phase.

Completing the exercises in this book will mean you have followed a well thought out methodology to work out what you want from your work and how you are going to go about achieving it. This should go a long way to reassuring you that you haven't rushed into a decision.

In order to maintain momentum or if you're getting stuck, you may want to look at working with a career coach. A good coach will tell you the things you don't necessarily want to hear, will challenge your thinking and will encourage you to stretch yourself. It is also important if the coaching relationship is going to be successful that you respect one another and enjoy working together. In Part Three we show you what to look out for if you do decide you want to find a career coach to work with.

If you are an organiser, something else you might consider is getting a small group of like-minded people together to work on this. You can use this book as a template, do the exercises on your own and get together weekly/monthly or whatever works for you to report back on progress and what you have discovered. You might also think about sharing the cost of a coach to facilitate the meetings with all of you – this could help keep the momentum going and provide you with a different viewpoint.

There are always options but for most people it is considerably easier to do this with support than on your own.

Mark credits his wife with being the impetus behind his career change and says he is quite sure that without her support and encouragement, he would still be a marketing controller, a job he hated but which paid the bills.

He had talked about having his own business but the time never seemed right to make the move so year after

year passed but nothing changed. When he mentioned to his wife that his new year's resolution was to start a business, she held him to it. He had two main options – either being a marketing freelancer or a photographer, something he'd always been passionate about. In the end, he combined the two.

It eventually took Mark 22 months to get his business up and running, setting up a sideline wedding photography business in the interim to test the market and bring in some additional income to pay for the transition. He did well and was soon winning enough business through referrals to make the business viable. He created a business plan, got himself a good accountant and joined all the professional photography organisations in his area.

He used his marketing background to help not only market his own photography business but also to join forces with other complementary businesses to create a joined up service of excellent professionals who specialised in weddings. He also works with two other businesses, one doing commercial photography and the other doing marketing consultancy.

His salary is about the same as it was before and the hours are longer but he has no doubt that his standard of living is substantially better. If it had not been for the support and occasional pushing of his wife, he says he would probably still be in a role he hated and wondering 'what if'.

Bringing people with you

Making a change in career direction may have ramifications for others as well as you. It is vital, at the outset, to find a way to bring them with you on this journey rather than merely presenting them with a change as a done deal. Having a frank conversation with a loved one can be a major stumbling block in the process and often the earlier such conversations take place the better.

Jordan had been working for his family's business since he left university but he had never felt particularly settled there. He worked his way through the exercises and made the decision to retrain as a sports injury therapist. He did all his research, spoke to therapists about their jobs and found out how he could retrain; he had even been accepted on a course. Then he came to a halt. The thing he had been avoiding was no longer avoidable. He had to tell his parents he was planning on leaving their business and would not be taking it over on their retirement. He practised the conversation over and over before finally sitting down with them and talking them through his decision. They were surprised that he had done so much without mentioning it but after that initial surprise were wholly supportive – something he had not expected.

Bite the bullet and have the conversation. Work out what you want to say, perhaps do some research ahead of time so that you are not talking in broad brush terms about important things like how you'll be able to pay the bills and don't be surprised if they may need some time to assimilate what you've said. For you, this is something you have had plenty of time to think about – for them, this may come out of the blue so give them some time to react and then think about it.

Mike had been looking for a job in his field of expertise for 18 months following redundancy and despite his best efforts had been unsuccessful. His research and efforts had been exhaustive – he knew every employer in his field, he knew every recruiter who specialised in what he did and he had applied for everything he could. He was stuck. During coaching, it became clear that there was an 'elephant in the room' that he was not talking about. It emerged that his wife had told him when he lost his job that he had 18 months to find a new one or they were going to go back and live in her native Wales and become self sufficient – his idea of hell. His 18 months was up, he was incredibly nervous and so avoided the conversation and was deliberately vague with his wife about his job search. After much coaxing, he brought up the subject of the deadline with his wife who looked surprised and then amused. She told him that she had said what she did to try and spur him on, knowing that he would hate it; she had no intention of moving away from their lives in London if they could possibly help it. Mike felt like a huge weight had been lifted from his shoulders and returned to his job search with a different attitude. He had two job offers a month later. Clearly, that could have been a coincidence but Mike is convinced that once that 'sword of Damocles' was no longer over his head, he came across very differently.

Whoever you feel you should bring on side in your career search, do it sooner rather than later!

8. How to decide on a direction

'A journey of a thousand miles begins with a single step.'
CONFUCIUS, Chinese thinker and social philosopher

With so many career options available it is easy to become paralysed with indecision. Combined with the fact that there is a lot of emotion attached to choosing a new career path, it can feel like it will be difficult to make a rational, well thought out decision. We have spent a decade researching and developing the methodology that is outlined in Part Two and Part Three to make it as streamlined, practical and achievable as possible. We know from experience that by taking a systematic approach, gathering information, researching and undertaking due diligence, that leaps of faith feel less daunting.

There are many ways to dip your toe into new waters as we saw with Henry Teare earlier. He worked at the weekends and did a great deal of research to see whether his chosen new field was the right one. Working through this book will help you to get enough real information about you and the job market you are interested in, and help you define the action steps required, to make a move to lessen that risk as far as is possible.

We are keen to emphasise that this is a journey – often it doesn't go in a straight line from A to B but should be regarded as an ongoing process. If you are ready to take the journey with us, turn to Part Two and let's start building the foundations of your new career direction.

PART TWO: UNDERSTANDING YOURSELF AND WHAT YOU WANT

'The life that is unexamined is not worth living.'

PLATO, Greek philosopher

The purpose of Part Two is to create a framework for your thinking and provide a structure to gather information relevant to your career. The result will give you an overview of who you are and what you want from work. Before you start protesting that you don't have time for this bit – there is no getting around the information gathering! And don't even think of outsourcing this as only YOU know the answers! Over the last 10 years we have tested a variety of different exercises and the ones listed in this section have worked successfully for our clients. Occasionally, clients need to do some more work on understanding themselves and so we have provided some further resources (see Chapter 18 in Part Two) to use in case you become stuck.

In Part One, we highlighted how important momentum is to success and in Part Two, this is going to become vital. As you complete each exercise, sorting through your work and life memories for examples, you may feel your enthusiasm waning. These exercises can be time consuming and from experience we know that completing them is one of those things that most people tell us they are tempted to put off until tomorrow. We hate to point out the obvious but the longer you put it off, the longer this whole process is going to take!

Follow each step of the process; you may think you already have a sense of your main skills or values but each step has been designed as a stepping stone to the next so it is important to follow each of them through. Just like building a wall, you can count on it being the brick you have left out that will be the vital one in making the whole thing stable and useful. The reason for gathering the information in this format is that you can pull it together in a matrix which will make up the components of the ideal job for you at this point in your life.

The quality of the answers to the questions in Part Two, i.e. the more information you gather in a clear and focused way and the more thought you put into it, means the more likely you are to glean the best results.

If any of the exercises seem particularly daunting, try breaking them down into manageable chunks so that you do not become intimidated by what we are asking you to do or the time you think it is going to take. If you wait for that 'clear' weekend where you can sit down and do the whole lot, it may never happen!

One of the things that we tell clients at the outset of the coaching relationship is that the methodology is not rocket science and that when we look back at it, much of it will feel like common sense. It has a beginning, middle and an end and is based on the premise that the more real information you have, the easier it is to make decisions and move towards change.

Keep a career folder

It is a good idea to keep all the information you gather in one place. Storing your information in a box file or folder will make it easier to find and many of our clients refer to their career folder periodically as their careers develop.

If you would find it easier to download printable versions of the exercises, then please go to **www.howtotakechargeofyourcareer.com** where you will find all the exercises.

While it is always useful to spend time **thinking** about the various aspects that we will cover in this part of the book, there is no substitute for **writing** things down, which has been proven to be so much more effective. Our clients are often surprised about how much more information they come up with when they get it down on paper.

We will look at your past and present experience, and ask, What is important to you now? We will then look at your aspirations for the future. This will all draw together to give as complete a picture as possible to use as our basis for brainstorming options for your future career.

So let's kick this off by looking at what you already know from your experience to date (regardless of whether you have work experience or not!).

9. Defining your top skills and strengths

'When love and skill work together, expect a masterpiece.'
JOHN RUSKIN, English art critic and social thinker

The starting point for any potential future employer is what skills and expertise you can bring to the role he or she is interviewing you for. Knowing your key skills and strengths is crucial. Perhaps more important is being able to explain the context in which you have exhibited those skills so that you can explain them in a clear and concise way.

Even if you eventually set up your own business, this information will help you work out where your skill gaps are, which is crucial when hiring or partnering with other people.

In this section, we are going to look at all your talents (the ones that come naturally to you and the ones you have learned). Often when we think of our skills, we refer to what others have said that we are good at or we refer to our most recent job and list those skills. However, we also need to be aware of the skills that we were born with which are so often ignored. For example, if you are naturally chatty, then it may not make sense to work in a library but you may make a fantastic radio chat show host. If you are naturally extremely organised, how can you incorporate that into your new career?

What are you naturally good at doing? What do you have a knack for? We often find that these innate abilities are often overlooked and that our clients dismiss them, presuming that if they come easily to them, other people must find the same thing. It rarely occurs to us that the things that come naturally can be so difficult for others so whether you are naturally empathetic or can solve mathematical problems at the drop of the hat, it is important to recognise this. We have found that the skills that people have and that come easily to them often hold the clue as to a future career direction. Those who incorporate these natural talents into their everyday work life are often more successful, have more confidence and enjoy what they do. What they do feels like such a natural fit and they are recognised for their excellence. Never dismiss anything that you are good at as not relevant – it is important to think creatively about how you can harness what comes naturally to you and how it can work for you in your career, now and in the future.

When we talk about someone being talented at something, we lump together a huge number of skills and strengths. Madonna can be described as a pop star but when you break down all the aspects that this entails, it's a long list: vocal ability, performance skills, management skills, dance skills, rhythm, entrepreneurial spirit, fashion sense, ability to reinvent herself, energy, marketing skills – and so on. Rather than lumping together your respective talents, make sure you break them down into their component parts.

JANIE VAN HOOL CASE STUDY

From the age of six, I had only one ambition: I wanted to be an actress and nothing could persuade me from focusing on this goal every waking hour until I was accepted into RADA aged 19. After three exhilarating years in training there, I was ready to set foot into the business and make my way. I was lucky – I left there with a job, and although I didn't make my fortune, I earned enough from working across media to sustain myself as an actress and pay my bills.

The thing is, it didn't turn out to be quite as I had imagined it. I found filming really boring; commercials, although fantastically well paid, felt demeaning after three years of classical training; theatre meant endless travel by various unglamorous means of transport to set up in poorly attended, freezing theatres for almost no money. By the time I had my children, it was apparent that Kate Winslet's career was safe – I was never going to make it big and didn't really want to settle into the 'jobbing' niche I currently occupied. I was lucky – some instinct in me had told me that at 30, I would need a reality check. Was this the career I set out to achieve? Was I where I wanted to be? The answer for me at 30 was plainly, no, so I decided to change. A chance review of a programme one night at the theatre led me to take an MA in Voice and train to teach voice and dialects to actors and business people. I now run a successful teaching practice helping people create presence and make an impact professionally. The skills I learned as an actress are incredibly useful and I've found I can use these practical skills to make a real difference to clients, which I love.

The biggest challenge I had in making the change was the grief of letting go of my childhood hopes and dreams, although I'm more successful and fulfilled now than I have ever been. It still took a couple of years to acknowledge that.

I would definitely make a change again in the future – I'm already working towards it. My advice to anyone would be to keep reviewing – are you where you want to be? Getting what you want? As long as you know your USP (Unique Selling Point), you can transfer your skills. It's challenging, invigorating and makes you realise what you're capable of.

Skills exercises

Stage 1 – What skills were you born with?

In addition to the more formal exercises, we have some questions for you that may just help spark an idea or thought that won't be captured in any other way. Remember to add the information from the exercises to your career folder.

Skills and talents: things to consider

What knacks do you have? What has always come easily to you at school, home, family, work, socially?

What do you most enjoy doing? What do others consider a chore but you really enjoy?

What do you find difficult that seems to come easily to other people? What are your blind spots?

Are you drawn to people or things?

Are you results oriented or do you enjoy being part of a greater whole where the final outcome is not as important to you?

Do you need to be right or are you happy working with possibilities and abstracts? Do you enjoy solving problems or would prefer to avoid them?

Are you future focused?

Are you physically dexterous?

Do you like to solve problems with other people or by yourself?

Do you enjoy finding connections in the previously unconnected? Do you think laterally? Do you like analysing issues or solving logical puzzles?

Do you enjoy generating new ideas?

Do you use your gut feelings/your intuition?

Are you a quick thinker?

Are you action oriented?

Do you enjoy working with the minutiae of a job, ensuring that every last 'i' is dotted, or do you tend to focus on the big picture?

Are you people oriented when making decisions? Can you identify how people are feeling? Are you more likely to analyse the logical consequences of a decision?

Are you able to adapt your style to suit someone you are engaging with?

Do you have an aptitude for languages?

Are you creative? (This can mean many things to many people e.g. able to think outside of the box, inventive, or good at generating new ideas.)

Do you have artistic ability in any form (music, art, writing)?

Do you prefer to be organised or live in a more spontaneous way?

List the top 5 skills you were born with:

1.

2.

3.

4.

5.

Stage 2 – Proving you have those skills

This next exercise has a dual purpose. Firstly it will help you understand your top skills, the ones you enjoy using and would like to use in the future. Most people can do many different jobs so the challenge is to find something you enjoy. Others are able to do an excellent job despite not enjoying their work; imagine how powerful they would be if they used their skills to do something they *did* enjoy? So rather than concentrate on **all** of your skills we will focus primarily on the ones you are particularly good at and enjoy – a powerful combination.

Secondly, knowing and having evidence of your top skills is key to the career assessment process. For example, it's not enough to say that you have 'great communication skills,' you also need to be able to answer questions such as:

> *'Describe a situation when you have presented ideas to a group in a persuasive manner?'*

This kind of question is increasingly used at interview and is called a 'competency-based' or 'behavioural' interview question. It can be difficult for an interviewer to work out competencies like 'communication skills' from CVs, as your experience can only allude to the skill and in most cases there won't be any hard evidence.

Step 1:

Think of times in your life when you have really enjoyed doing something and were good at it, the times when you felt immersed in what you were doing and were proud of the results.

Jog your memory by getting out an old CV, listing all the jobs you have ever done (paid and not paid) or looking back through photograph albums. What did you get commended for, both inside and outside work? What did you really enjoy doing? Also think back over your home life and education in the same way, and analyse your achievements. If very little comes to you at first, write down as much as you can, then leave it and come back to it – take your time. Try to think of actual examples and give as much detail as possible. We ask you to analyse these stories in this format as it is how many recruiters want to see evidence of your skills.

Competency-based questions

When answering interview questions, it is useful to use the STAR method which is:

S – Situation – what was the context in which you used your skills?
T – Task – what was the challenge?
A – Action – what was the action you took?
R – Result – what was the result?

Below is an example taken from outside work; it is always important to think about such events in your life too as they will highlight your different skills as much as work-related events.

What was the Situation? My best friend's 30th birthday

What was the Task you had to undertake? Organise her birthday party without her knowledge

What was the Action you took?

- Contacted a small group of friends/her family to agree on the type of party, location, how we were going to pay for it and the guest list
- Sent out invitations to everyone she would want at the event having 'obtained' her address books and social networking contacts
- Arranged for overnight accommodation for guests who needed it
- Found a venue and organised entertainment for the night (including music, food, drink, photographer, transport to and from the event)
- Devised an intricate plan to get to her to the party without her realising what was going on (including arranging an outfit, makeover etc.) so that she would arrive feeling a million dollars
- Sorted out the finance for the event and made sure everyone knew what they would have to contribute ahead of time so this aspect ran smoothly
- Acted as MC for the event and arranged speeches and a slide show of pictures from her past
- Following the event, put together a book of photographs of the evening as her final present

What was the Result you got? It was a fantastic party that everyone enjoyed. My friend was very touched and excited to have a birthday party arranged for her. She couldn't believe that she had absolutely no idea what was going on until she arrived.

If you are struggling to come up with ideas for this section, you could ask a friend or family member who might help you jog your memory, encourage you and give an objective viewpoint.

Try to come up with five stories of your own using the STAR method. You can fill in your first one here:

What was the Situation?

What was the Task you had to undertake?

What was the Action you took?

What was the Result you got?

James found this exercise a struggle. 'I had been warned that this would take me quite a while to do but it was hard to find the motivation to keep going. I struggled to come up with a list of things I was proud of having achieved and deciding which stories to expand was difficult – was I getting it right? I'm pleased I stuck with it though because although the list wasn't hugely different to a general skills list I would have pulled together myself, having stories to back up those skills has proved invaluable in interview situations. The hard work was worth it."

Step 2:

Go through the following list of skills for each story and ask yourself the question, 'Can I prove that I have acquired these skills in each of the above situations?' If so, tick the corresponding box. Once you have done the initial review, you can refine the list especially if you find that for a particular situation you have ticked several words that effectively mean the same thing.

For each story – I displayed the ability to:

Skill	Place a tick by the skills in which you have both a strength and which you enjoy.
Act	
Adapt	
Administrate	
Advertise	
Analyse	
Arbitrate	
Assist	
Assess	
Audit	
Brainstorm	
Budget	
Build relationships	
Calculate	
Coach	

Collaborate	
Collect	
Communicate in writing	
Communicate verbally	
Communicate fluently in a foreign language	
Compile	
Compose	
Compute	
Conceptualise	
Conduct	
Consolidate	
Consult	
Contract	
Construct	
Contribute	
Coordinate	
Delegate	
Deliver	
Demonstrate	
Design	
(be) Detail oriented	
Develop ideas	
Develop new business	
Discover	
Distribute	
Document	
Draft	
Educate	
Empathise	
Employ	
Examine	
Enforce	
Engineer	
Enhance	

Entertain	
Establish	
Evaluate	
Execute	
Experiment	
Explain	
Explore	
Facilitate	
Finance	
Forecast	
Formulate	
Fundraise	
Gather information	
Generate ideas	
Give appropriate feedback	
Handle complaints	
Handle details	
Identify problems	
Identify resources	
Illustrate	
Implement	
Improve	
Improve processes	
Improvise	
Influence	
Innovate	
Inspect	
Inspire	
Interpret	
Interview	
Invent	
Investigate	
Keep detailed records	
Judge	
Lead	

Learn	
Listen	
Make decisions	
Market	
Manage a team	
Manage change	
Manage conflict	
Manage time	
Manage information	
Mediate	
Mentor	
Model	
Monitor	
Motivate	
Multitask	
Negotiate	
Network	
Observe	
Organise	
Overhaul	
Partner with	
Perceive patterns	
Pioneer	
Plan	
Plan and run events	
Predict	
Present	
Present/Act/Deliver	
Prioritise	
Problem solve	
Programme	
Project manage	
Promote change	
Publicise	
Question	

Reason	
Recommend	
Recruit	
Repair	
Research	
Review	
Save time	
Save money	
Save resources	
Sell ideas	
Sell products	
Set goals	
Set and meet deadlines	
Standardise	
Support others	
Teach	
Team build	
Think laterally	
Train	
Volunteer	
Other:	
Other:	
Other:	
Other:	
Other:	

Which are the skills which get the highest number of ticks? List the top five here:

1.

2.

3.

4.

5.

Step 3: Consolidate your findings

Referring to the five skills above, write a sentence that details your real and specific strength. For example you may state communication as one of your top skills – but what makes you stand out is your ability to communicate clearly and in a motivational way in tough situations. This can help you work out where to focus this skill.

My strength in skill 1 is:

My strength in skill 2 is:

My strength in skill 3 is:

My strength in skill 4 is:

My strength in skill 5 is:

We ask you to consider your skills in this way as it highlights when your answer is too vague and really makes you think about the evidence of your top skills. There may be some crossover between your 'born skills' and the skills you have solid evidence for – that's fine. It's important to look at them all.

Finally, it is important to consider your skills in relation to the market:

- Do your skills have long-term currency as you progress in your career or might you need to develop these skills further?
- Are your skills becoming obsolete in the market?

10. What do you value?

*'When your values are clear to you,
making decisions becomes easier.'*
ROY DISNEY, Director of the Walt Disney Corporation

We often find that this is something that most of our clients have spent little, if any, time thinking about although when we start to explore what they value in their lives and work environments, they recognise that knowing what is important to them is key. Having said that, values are something that most of us don't build into the equation when we are looking at careers but they can serve as a useful focus or reference point for all aspects of our life.

We define work values as 'those interests and qualities which you feel are important in your work'. Obviously your work values are highly likely to overlap with your personal values but it is useful to have a think about whether your life is aligned with the things you say are important to you. This is one area which can change radically as you have more life experiences or life changes (e.g. having a family to consider).

It may not be necessary to orient your life entirely around your values; however, it will be possible (and rewarding) to weave them into most aspects of your life.

Acting as a reference point, values can help you to:

- set clear goals for the future that are worthwhile and are important to you;
- improve the quality of your decisions;
- maintain your confidence when you feel confused or when you're in a period of transition.

We suggest you redo this exercise every year. Your values can change with your life circumstances so it is important to ensure that your life is in line with your current values rather than those of five years ago.

GARY BOYD CASE STUDY

I didn't shine or even glow warmly at school. I was broadly average at everything I did, neither excelling nor failing. Nothing wrong with that but not the great egalitarian social climbing story I'd imagined. I wanted to go to university, however, with changes to grants I couldn't afford to. My family wouldn't support me unless I did a 'proper' degree and I had a yearning to study English and drama. They said they'd support me if I did something useful, so I did something useful. I successfully completed the civil service exams and joined their middle management ranks straight from school. I managed a few temporary promotions, worked for the relevant trade union and happily carried this on for eight or so years. Although not a shining light in the world of the civil service I was relatively successful and, given the TU activism, I was reasonably satisfied with my job.

If there was a catalyst for my career change it came only indirectly from my pen pushing. I worked in an office that was next to a school in north London and with the magnificence of flexitime I began to read with groups of children before their lunch. This was weekly, then daily and, stretching flexitime to its stretchy limit, I began reading and helping out before and after the school lunch break. I loved it. I wanted to be a teacher but didn't have a degree and did have a mortgage. I became increasingly happier in the school than in the office but the office paid better. I applied through UCAS for a degree in education in the mid-nineties after eighteen months' volunteering. However, I needed a reason to pack in my job. I was in a relatively comfortable position so had to seek a reason to jump in at the deep end and become a 26-year-old undergraduate – there weren't many mature students in those days. I think my justification for escape was born of my TU activism and I had a significant reason to leave after representing someone at a Civil Service Appeals Board. The individual had been dismissed for being grossly incompetent but the dismissing manager, in an act of equal incompetence, had failed to follow the correct procedures and the worker was reinstated. The worker phoned me up and demanded that either I or the union solicitors pursue a claim for compensation on top of his reinstatement. I went to work the next day and gave notice that I would be leaving to become a teacher the following September. It was January and places were not yet allocated at universities but I knew I had to go.

AUTONOMY

- ❑ Autonomy
- ❑ Personal authority
- ❑ Independence

CREATIVITY

- ❑ Individuality
- ❑ Unpredictability
- ❑ Expedience
- ❑ Originality
- ❑ Ingenuity
- ❑ Freedom
- ❑ Creativity

ENTREPRENEURIAL

- ❑ Risk
- ❑ Adventure
- ❑ Experiment
- ❑ Dynamism
- ❑ Competition
- ❑ Energy
- ❑ Innovation
- ❑ Novelty
- ❑ Entrepreneurial zeal

EXPERTISE

- ❑ Expertise
- ❑ Technical expertise
- ❑ Proficiency
- ❑ Superiority
- ❑ Competence

INTELLECT

- ❑ Education
- ❑ Intellectual challenge
- ❑ Intellectual stimulation

LIFESTYLE/WORK BALANCE

- ❑ Lively
- ❑ Fun
- ❑ Choice
- ❑ Flexibility
- ❑ Good work/life balance

FINANCIAL REWARD	POWER AND INFLUENCE
❑ Profit	❑ Guidance
❑ Pay and bonuses	❑ Governance
❑ Financial freedom	❑ Power
❑ Building financial value	❑ Influence

RECOGNITION	SECURITY
❑ Respect	❑ Predictability
❑ Reward	❑ Safety
❑ Praise	❑ Security
❑ Recognition	❑ Stability
❑ Appreciation	❑ Regularity

STRUCTURE	YOUR OWN
❑ Structure	❑
❑ Organisation	❑
❑ Order	❑
❑ Clarity	❑
❑ Efficiency	❑
	❑

Step 2:

Now that you have your preliminary list (your ticked 'values'), this will help you to rank your values in order of importance.

List your 10 values in the column on the left hand side of the grid on the page (see pages 66 and 67 for a blank DecidingValues Grid). To decide which value is most important, compare each pair of values and and circle the number relating to the value you decide on. When arriving at your decision ask yourself, If I could only say one of these was true for my chosen career, which would I prefer? Try not to think what others might say or think about you, be brutally honest with yourself.

Once you have completed the whole grid you need to add up the number of times you have circled each value and enter it in the corresponding box in the 'number of circles' line at the bottom of the grid.

This will help you determine the ranking of your values. Allocate 1–10 to your values according to the number of times you have circled them.

Enter the rankings into the 'final ranking' line at the bottom of the grid. You can now enter your prioritised values in the right-hand column of the grid.

These can be used as your reference point for any job-hunting activities or career decisions you are required to make.

For a completed example of the deciding values grid, see pages 64 and 65.

EXAMPLE OF DECIDING VALUES

Your 10 Values					
1 Autonomy	V1				
2 Expertise	1 ②	V2			
3 Flexibility	1 ③	② 3	V3		
4 Money	1 ④	② 4	③ 4	V4	
5 Governance	① 5	② 5	③ 5	④ 5	V5
6 Influence	1 ⑥	② 6	③ 6	④ 6	5 ⑥
7 Reward	1 ⑦	② 7	③ 7	④ 7	5 ⑦
8 Structure	① 8	② 8	③ 8	④ 8	⑤ 8
9 Respect	1 ⑨	2 ⑨	3 ⑨	4 ⑨	5 ⑨
10 Education	1 ⑩	② 10	3 ⑩	④ 10	5 ⑩

1	2	3	4	5
2	8	6	6	1
#8	#2	#3	#3	#9

					Prioritised Values
					1 Respect
					2 Expertise
					3 Flexibility
					3 Money
					5 Education
V6					6 Influence
6 7	V7				7 Reward
6 8	7 8	V8			8 Autonomy
6 9	7 9	8 9	V9		9 Governance
6 10	7 10	8 10	9 10	V10	9 Structure

6	7	8	9	10	Item number
4	3	1	9	5	Number of circles
#6	#7	#9	#1	#5	Final Rank

DECIDING VALUES

Your 10 Values					
1	V(value)1				
2	1 2	V2			
3	1 3	2 3	V3		
4	1 4	2 4	3 4	V4	
5	1 5	2 5	3 5	4 5	V5
6	1 6	2 6	3 6	4 6	5 6
7	1 7	2 7	3 7	4 7	5 7
8	1 8	2 8	3 8	4 8	5 8
9	1 9	2 9	3 9	4 9	5 9
10	1 10	2 10	3 10	4 10	5 10

1	2	3	4	5

					Prioritised Values
					1
					2
					3
					4
					5
V6					6
6 7	V7				7
6 8	7 8	V8			8
6 9	7 9	8 9	V9		9
6 10	7 10	8 10	9 10	V10	10

6	7	8	9	10	Item number
					Number of circles
					Final rank

11. What are your interests and passions?

'When I work, I relax. Doing nothing...makes me tired.'
PABLO PICASSO, Spanish painter

Interests can be a major factor in your career. They can help you decide which industry to target or what type of business to set up. Working in an industry or business which incorporates your interests can make you feel motivated to work harder, and usually results in increased job satisfaction. Having said that, sometimes interests should stay as hobbies! Perhaps there is no way to make them commercially viable or maybe they bring in some income but not enough to support you full-time.

A lot of the people we work with don't know what they are really interested in. It is very important to start to become more aware of what holds your interest (i.e. having an 'explorer's mindset') and what bores you to tears. This is different for different people – while racing cars might fascinate you, they may bore me. With our recruiter's hat on, we can see when someone is passionate about what they do, their eyes sparkle; they are animated when talking about it and the energy just radiates from them. Often this passion will set them apart from the rest and when employed, they will have the energy to go the 'extra mile' and give 100 per cent to everything they do. It may take some soul-searching and time to find industries you are interested in but it is time well spent as it will mean your career has more longevity.

So how do you get in touch with what you are interested in and then evaluate whether it should form part of your career plan? First you need to increase your awareness and the first step is to answer the questions below.

Interests exercise

Answer the questions below and consider whether your interests could form part of your career. Try and be as specific as you can. If business interests you, what part of business? Sales? Human Resources?

Try and break it down further – if it is Human Resources, is that recruitment, compensation and benefits or training?

The last couple of questions focus around industry sector. We ask these questions because it helps to also target sectors which you are interested in and that may be growing, thus offering more opportunity.

1. What do you do in your leisure time?
2. Are you passionate about any of your interests?
3. Do you have knowledge or relative expertise in an area that you have built up, just because you are interested in it?
4. What books or magazines do you read? If you went into a bookshop, what sections would you look in?
5. What section of the newspaper do you turn to first?
6. Have you ever volunteered for work or assignments?
7. Are you interested in any particular industry sector?
8. Which industry sectors do you think are growing or have potential for growth?

It can be useful to keep coming back to this section and adding things that pique your interest. Add articles to your career folder. Make a note of films, TV or radio programmes that make you think and interest you – what is it about them that caught your interest?

Some clients can be downhearted if they can't seem to find one thing that really ignites their passion. This is not unusual but don't give up. Keep looking out for fields that pique your interest and do some research to find out more about them – it can sometimes be an aspect to the field that you haven't come across before that contains the key to a new direction. Look at anything that interests you – is it chatting to friends, cooking desserts, researching holiday destinations, finding out about family history? Start researching options that might work with those interests and you might be able to creatively combine different fields of interest in your work and personal life, perhaps by adopting a portfolio career.

George was always passionate about music. He was the founder and Music Director of his college when he was at University. After a degree in natural sciences he went into the city as a financial analyst at Hill Samuel. Following an MBA from the Tuck School of Management he joined Cargill, an international producer and marketer of food, agricultural and industrial products, as a high flying manager, and eventually became a Director responsible for Strategy and Business Development. With a young family he was tired of travelling constantly and in his mind he had a burning desire to combine his skills with his first love – music.

After following the career change process, he seized the opportunity to become Head of Commercial Development at Glyndebourne Opera. This has necessitated a lifestyle change for George, but with his family supporting his decision he successfully made the transition and uses his business skills in a field which he is much more passionate about.

Finding evidence of your passion

It is all very well to say you are 'passionate' about a field but you need to gather evidence that it is a viable option – not only for the employer if you are going for interview but also for yourself if you are changing career; George could draw on his lifelong interest in music which is evidenced by his early achievements at university.

From our experience as recruiters and those we speak to regularly, the importance of collecting evidence of your interest in a new career is key. This may include some of the following:

- Unpaid work or voluntary work full-time, part-time or in your spare time – you don't have to say it was unpaid on your CV!
- Consultancy or contract work to gain experience
- Involvement in clubs or associations connected with your interest

Find a way to get your foot in the door

Working with a career coach, Steve identified the key skills that would be attractive to an employer and the subjects that he was passionate about. When combined, Steve's research pointed to a career in the commercial side of the sports industry. It was a small field and operated on a 'who you know' basis. Through leveraging his limited contacts to make new ones he eventually secured his first role at a sports management company, which was the foot in the door he needed.

People working as a consultant or on a contract are very attractive to employers, as they are much lower risk to hire than those joining the firm through traditional recruitment channels like advertising. Employers have seen first hand the quality of their work and how they fit into the team – the best 'interview' there is! It also means the employer saves substantially on recruitment fees which can vary from anything from 15-33 per cent of annual salary.

Complete a course or enhance your knowledge about your field

Charlotte had gone into interior design after a history degree at university. She found interior design stifling and realised it didn't stretch her intellectually. Not knowing what she wanted to do, frustrated and confused as to what career to follow she went travelling but returned a year later no further on in her thinking.

After completing the skills exercise (see Chapter 9 in Part Two) she discovered that while she had been in interior design she had particularly enjoyed putting client records on to a database she had designed. She had a fledgling interest in IT and decided to do a six-week evening course to see if this interest was just a passing phase or something more substantial. After the course she discovered her interest had grown and she felt motivated to move into this field. She received several offers from IT graduate recruitment schemes, despite, at 27, being older than the majority of people on such schemes. She accepted an offer from Thames Water and the HR Manager who interviewed her said one of the main reasons the company offered her the job was that she had clearly worked through a structured career assessment and they felt she had done her 'career change' homework. She was not a 'risk' because she had proven evidence of her interest in the IT field.

Charlotte took a short course to test her interest in this relatively new field. Attending events such as conferences and reading the industry press can ensure you come across as knowledgeable; several clients have been hired after meeting people at industry events. This insider's knowledge can improve the questions you ask and make you appear that you have been in the industry for ages. Once you have overcome the initial hurdle of making contact and appearing to be knowledgeable about the industry you are seeking to join, then sometimes a lack of experience can be over looked.

Include project work as part of your course if you are doing a further education qualification

Many MBA and Master's students use projects and internships to gain experience that then serves as vital evidence of interest in a new field. Sometimes projects can be carefully planned so that there is an opportunity to talk to different companies and to people who could potentially hire you.

Robin used his MBA project in internal change management at a major oil company to make the transition into consultancy. While working on the project he came into contact with several consultancy firms; he interviewed with a couple before finally joining one of them. Since then he has transferred to the Perth office to combine his management consultancy career with the outdoor lifestyle he had identified as a passion.

Travel

Many people take gap years or travel breaks, often as an escape from a job or because they are not sure what to do next. Used carefully, travel can help you to gain experience in a certain field, for example working on an English newspaper in a foreign country might be useful if you were looking to gain journalism experience. If you do go travelling, future employers may want to know what you got out of it, so it's always useful to keep that in mind – what experiences might show a new aspect of your personality or a key area of competence?

Tom didn't enjoy being a solicitor and after working through these exercises, he decided to pursue his interest in wine. Having originally planned to go travelling to 'escape' his solicitor job, after he worked with Camilla, he decided to use his travel time in Australia to do some research into the wineries there. He spent several months talking to people in the trade and researching the types of roles available in the industry. He came back even more determined to enter the wine trade. He sold his house to release some equity to live on while he took a radical pay cut to work in a local wine shop, gaining experience while he took his wine exams. Over the years he has steadily progressed within the wine trade and despite the drop in income compared with a career in the law, he has never regretted his move.

Some people, like Christine Rucker from the White Company, have developed a business around their passion, in her case, interior design. For others this can be a mistake. Just because you love golf for example doesn't necessarily mean you would love running a golfing shop – the day-to-day running of a shop or even a chain of shops is not necessarily the same as the buzz you get from playing or watching golf on TV. This is why it is important to consider your interests and passions not in isolation but in relation to the other career elements such as skills, values, work environments etc. You may be able to weave interests and hobbies into your life in other ways: Mark, for example, decided that while he was passionate about climbing and skiing, the types of full-time roles open to him would not meet his financial requirements. He ended up relocating to New Zealand, where staying in the same field of IT let him pursue his passion for mountain sports.

LINDSAY SMALL CASE STUDY

Although I went to a good university, I found academic study very frustrating. I wanted to be out in the world, and at that time the City was the place to be. I took the secretarial route into the City then managed to move from that into investment research – writing my own research as an analyst and then editing other people's research. Editing quickly became a passion: I was good at it, and I loved the City environment.

It was my decision to have children that provoked a career change. I wasn't prepared to work full-time City hours, and in those days there wasn't any leeway. Although it was my decision, I found life at home with the kids a real challenge at first: I was a fish out of water in the playground and I missed almost everything about the City.

To maintain my interests over the next few years, I started three small businesses. It was the start-up which really interested me; they never held my interest once they were up and running. They brought in a little income and experience but most importantly I learned something about myself and my strengths and weaknesses with each new venture, and that process ultimately allowed me to discover my perfect business arena – the Internet.

Almost the first time I went online I realised that I had found my perfect field. When my youngest child started school I began work on a website for parents and teachers of young children. It took off very quickly, and now, nine years later, over one million people visit that website every month. I have a portfolio of additional 'family friendly websites' helped by various freelancers, and I earn a very good income from my sites. I still find new challenges to keep me interested and motivated, and I am able to work completely around my family.

Would I change my career again? Absolutely, as long as I was working for myself! There are so many things that I would like to have a go at, and I still have new ideas almost every day. These days so many people get stuck in one unfulfilling career because firms want specialists and good specialists are encouraged to stay in that specialty forever. But that doesn't mean you can't do something else – or 100 other things, given the time and the inclination! And if your first attempt isn't perfect for you, learn from it, examine your strengths and weaknesses, and move on to the next…

12. What is your ideal working environment?

'You are a product of your environment. So choose the environment that will best develop you toward your objective. Analyse your life in terms of its environment. Are the things around you helping you toward success – or are they holding you back?'

W. CLEMENT STONE, American author

You now have a comprehensive list of your transferable skills, values and interests to capitalise on in your next role. Continuing the theme of looking to what you know about yourself from experience, next we are going to look at common themes that have surfaced about what you like and dislike in a work environment. Don't panic if you don't have a huge amount of work experience to draw upon, any information is useful.

Many of us will have been in an environment which was toxic to us and not conducive to doing our best work. It's very important you take the time to recognise what environment to avoid in the future and what to seek out. This focus can be of interest to a potential employer who, in our experience, is impressed by someone who has taken the time to ensure they are joining the right environment for them – a form of due diligence. It shows you take your career seriously and that you understand the best environment for you. We also know that potential employers and recruiters are impressed when a candidate has taken the time to speak to other people in the firm to find out what it is really like to work there. This reduces the risk of a candidate joining and then leaving because there isn't a good 'fit' and makes both the recruiter and the candidate look good.

Environment exercise

For each job you have held in the past, describe as fully as possible those factors which made that job especially exciting or rewarding (i.e. those things you liked) and those elements that made it especially boring or frustrating (i.e. things you disliked). Be as specific as possible.

Examples to consider might include:

- Office (was it open plan, did you have your own office, was it light and airy)
- Colleagues (were they social, interactive, team oriented, quiet)
- Remuneration (pay, benefits such as holiday, canteen, pension)
- Promotion prospects
- Sense of freedom (did you work out of the office, were you micromanaged)
- Style of management (open to suggestion, hierarchical, collegiate, supportive)
- Development (were development opportunities offered e.g. coaching, mentoring, training)
- Why are you (thinking about) no longer working there?
- What was it about the role that made you want to take it on?
- How did it live up to expectations?
- How did it fail to live up to expectations?
- Do you thrive in a big company environment? Would you be better suited to a smaller company?

JOB	LIKED	DISLIKED

When Megan first did this exercise, she did a quick brainstorm of ideas so she could get to the next section. When she came to review it later, she started to see the first signs of some common themes such as having autonomy in her work life, not being tied to her job nine-to-five and being with sparky individuals who believed in something. This was the starting point for her brainstorming and she's now working with an SME where there is huge freedom to contribute to a product that all staff feel passionately about.

Your ideal environment

This list of likes and dislikes should give you an idea of what to look for and what to avoid when you are considering approaching certain firms. Take the three most important elements of your ideal work environment and list them below.

1.

2.

3.

ANNE WILLIAMS CASE STUDY

The turning point for me came when I returned to work after the birth of my first child, as a project manager for a high profile, strategic redesign business improvement project. This gave me exposure to management consultants and I instinctively knew that their world was far more 'me'. At that time my world was one-dimensional and it was then that I intuitively understood that I needed to complete an MBA to equip me with the skills for a future career challenge and change.

After several false starts post MBA, where…I ended up working for organisations with work environments that ignored bad management practices, I learnt that at interview it was crucial for me to go into a lot of detail about an average day to make a decision about whether it was right for me – just because they want you doesn't mean the job's right for you!

I am now about to start working for one of the world's top five management consultancies. Will it work for me? I think so, but why do I believe that I have got it right this time? Firstly, I was overtly 'me' during the recruitment process which entailed four one-to-one interviews, three psychometric tests and a role play, in an attempt to test the boundaries of the personality/culture fit. This didn't seem to set off any alarm bells; if anything it was the reverse. The more I came out of my shell, the more successful I was. It appears that my critical insight was an asset not a threat; my intellect and academic achievement was an advantage not a hindrance; my gregarious nature and sense of fun was a key tool in networking and maintaining visibility rather than a distraction and a nuisance. Will it work? Who really knows, but I think it will. Many of my colleagues and friends are keen to point out to me that this is exactly what I should have done years ago, that it suits me and my skills best. Either way, I am not worried anymore, because I know that if it is not for me, I *am* good enough and the search must go on. All that it needed, like finding your life partner, is that 'right fit'.

My one piece of advice is always strive for that perfect personal 'fit', to have the confidence to craft and shape your life, being uncompromising and constantly questioning, so you can get the best out of it!

13. Your relationship with previous managers

'A good boss makes his men realise they have more ability than they think they have so that they consistently do better work than they thought they could.'

CHARLES ERWIN WILSON,
American businessman and politician

'I hate my boss!' is a familiar refrain for most people at some point during their working life. A great manager can support you, coach and develop you to be the best you can be. On the other hand a nightmare boss can belittle you, undermine you and wreck your confidence.

You may have mentioned your previous bosses/managers in the exercise you have just done but we want you to explore this a little more. Identifying why you didn't get on with certain managers and what traits you need in your manager to bring out the best in you are an important consideration when you are looking for a new role. If you've ever had a bad manager, you'll know exactly what we are talking about – they can make or break a job as many of our clients (us included!) have unfortunately found out.

Relationship with managers exercise

List below all the managers you have had in the past.

1.

2.

3.

4.

5.

(add more if needed)

When you look at that list, who did you work well for? Who would you cross the street to avoid now? Why? Knowing what you know about working for them, list the positive characteristics you are looking for in your next manager and the negative characteristics you are seeking to avoid:

Positive	Negative
e.g. supportive, bright, inclusive, fun, a role model	e.g. megalomaniac, stroppy, closed, micromanager

When Karen did this exercise, she was fascinated and surprised to see a common theme in the types of people she had worked for (all power hungry alpha personalities) who had never made her feel like she could achieve but were charismatic. When she was interviewing, she was offered two roles; she found it incredibly difficult to decide which way to go until she revisited this exercise. One of the roles would have involved working with another similar boss, the other was working for someone who was more focused on bringing her on in her new role. That was her decider and she's never looked back.

Finding out whether the environment or your manager is a good fit for you is down to your investigative abilities! You need to talk to people who work for the company, perhaps a friend of a friend who works there, as they may open up to you. Another way to check this out is to ask to meet the team for lunch or drinks after you have accepted an offer. That way you can ask some informal questions about the working environment to see if it really is for you.

14. Taking care of your needs

The majority of Part Two is looking at what we would like in an ideal working world – the skills we would like to use, the types of people we would like to work with, and so on. The one thing we must be careful not to overlook is your needs.

In 1943, Abraham Maslow developed his Hierarchy of Needs (see diagram below). As human beings, we start with our most basic needs at the bottom of the triangle and as we achieve each level of needs, we move up to the next level. It is perfectly possible to be moving through a couple of the levels at any one time. Where do you consider yourself to be right now? Are you striving to move to the higher levels and do you have a plan of how you hope to do that?

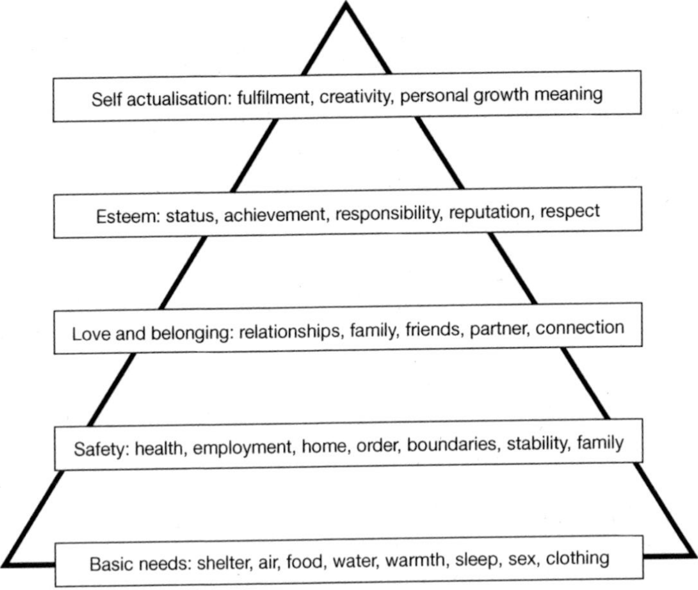

In terms of your next career move, have you considered what it is you **need** in order to make it more likely to work?

Needs exercise

List below the five main needs that you would like your future career to fulfil. Things you might want to consider are:

- job security;
- location;
- salary (give a range – both the minimum you can afford initially and the amount that will put a smile on your face);
- work constraints (hours you can work, ability to travel etc.);
- recognition;
- promotion prospects.

1.

2.

3.

4.

5.

After working out his budget and looking at all possible options, Peter knew he needed a certain basic salary to be able to keep up with his everyday bills such as mortgage, utilities, food etc. and without it he knew he would be panic stricken and struggle to function, even in a job he thought he would love. So he applied for, and got, a reduction of hours in his corporate job that would cover his main expenses and which left him with two days a week to pursue his new career as an upholsterer. Peter feels secure financially and is able to slowly build up his upholstery business. Although this has meant sacrificing potential career progression in his corporate role, it gives him an opportunity to check out the viability of his new career in a way that feels safe for him. Peter was honest about what his needs really were and adapted his plans to work for him. He had carefully considered what he would compromise on and what, categorically, he couldn't, which helped him make an informed decision.

15. What do I want out of life? Defining your long-term plan

'Don't wait. The time will never be just right.'
Napoleon Hill, American motivational writer on wealth

So far, we have looked at what you can learn from your past experiences and your present reality to help build a picture of what you are looking for in your ideal career path. Now we will look at your aspirations for the future and make sure that you factor in your hopes and dreams.

Clearly, nothing is written in stone. Life happens and your aspirations for the future will shift through changes in circumstances, both positive and negative. What we are looking for here is a snap shot of what you hope to achieve, not only in your career but in your life as a whole. Identifying your hopes may help with the brainstorming of possible job options in Chapter 17 and your aspirations may highlight a new path to explore.

A few years ago, Camilla worked with a client who had been in accounting for 10 years. He was bored and the idea of the rest of his career being more of the same with a few promotions along the way was demoralising. Having worked through all the exercises that you have now completed, a new direction had not presented itself and he was starting to lose hope that he would find the right role. Until, that was, he started looking into the future. He went through the next exercise filling in the information for each 10-year period until his fifties. Seemingly out of nowhere, his new career was to own a bistro with an art gallery attached where he could introduce his local community to young artists. However, in discussion, he said he felt it would only be possible to do that when he had made enough money to do what he really wanted as a 'hobby job'. As soon as he said it, the light bulb went on! He had found what he really wanted to do – now it was just a question of how to make it happen sooner. He had been persuaded by well-meaning teachers and parents to take up science rather than art at school and had never really considered the creative world as a possible job option although he still painted watercolours in his spare time. After much research and helping out at a local art gallery and museum at weekends, he retrained as an art restorer and is now working in an art gallery as a curator.

Sometimes, releasing the pressure of an immediate plan can show up some interesting ideas that you have played with in the back of your mind for years but have never thought possible. Now is the time to put that theory to the test through research and exploration and to find out whether your idea is a pipe dream or could be reality.

Most of us, when we talk about the future, tend not to think too far ahead – five years being the norm for those who have spent some time building long-term goals. Our clients rarely look at how their perspectives will change long term as they become older, perhaps move to the country or change their social habits – this section asks you to consider how old you will be, how old your children will be and to really put yourself in that place to answer the questions.

GORDON GREEN CASE STUDY

My first job was in the graduate programme of a major oil company after successfully completing a chemical engineering degree at university. I had no specific plan at the time and the programme certainly lived up to its reputation – I had assignments and gained valuable experience in many different parts of the organisation, coupled with lots of international travel and working very closely with the senior management. I thoroughly enjoyed my first few years but it was a double-edged sword as I began to feel that I wasn't in control of where my career was going – I was expected to move to different departments and locations at short notice and with no input.

Sensing my restlessness, the company sponsored me to do an MBA. Through the MBA, I met many like-minded people and started to have the confidence to shape my own career, instead of just allowing it to 'happen'.

My goal was to be self-employed so I would be able to choose my own lifestyle. But it also had to be a job which could bring me more satisfaction, in terms of tangible benefits to my life, and not just helping an organisation to be more profitable. And that's when I decided to be a lawyer.

However, to get there I needed to be financially secure as I appreciated the risks involved. So when I graduated from my MBA, I went into investment banking – being an investment banker not only provided enough mental challenges, but it also taught me how to work in an ultra-competitive environment with some of the brightest brains around. I thoroughly enjoyed my time in investment banking and the adrenaline rush that accompanied it. But more importantly I saved every penny of my bonuses in those few years as I knew it was an important step in my plan.

I did have my moment of doubt when I left investment banking – everybody was questioning the sanity of my decision. Why would one walk away from such a coveted job, with its pay and prestige? But I knew what I had in mind so I started doing my legal training part time, while using my previous experience in banking to get a job in a law firm, albeit in a non-legal capacity.

I undertook four years of part-time study while working full-time in one of the largest law firms in the world. It was not the easiest thing to do but it was all worth it as my future employer could see my seriousness in making a career change. So now I am well on my way to finishing my training to be a lawyer, and will soon to be able to work in an area I am interested in – human rights.

Looking back, I think one thing I have learned is that whatever you are doing now, and it may be something you do not enjoy, you are bound to be gaining skills and experience which will help you move on to the next step. It is important that, while you focus on your goals, you also make sure that you do not miss out on the important lessons you can learn from your current situation.

The other important point is to have patience – it's very easy to walk away from what you don't like and hope to make a complete change overnight. But it's equally important to bear in mind that many goals take a lot of planning and time to achieve; don't be put off by discouraging people who will tell you that you will be starting from the bottom of the ladder again, and you'll be older than most etc. These are usually people who are too afraid to make a change themselves.

Having an idea of your long-term goals will keep you focused on the bigger picture. This is important for several reasons:

- It will help with the career decisions you will inevitably have to make (e.g. deciding between two job options). It is much easier to make difficult choices if you are clear on your long-term goals.
- It will help you identify the skills you need to acquire or the actions you need to take to make your future aspirations a reality.
- Having a clear idea of where you are heading will give you additional drive to keep going towards your ultimate aim.

Setting interim and long-term goals is what helps create momentum and is something that so few of us do as a matter of course. If you are really considering what you want out of life, looking ahead is vital and we think these exercises are some of the most important in the book in helping to create your forward momentum. Without goals, you will find that your days, weeks, months and years get filled up with 'stuff' that aid the day-to-day living but when you look back, leave you wondering why you never really achieved what you had intended.

While here we are principally concerned with your career aspirations, goals in other parts of your life are important too so make sure they are compatible with each other.

Long-term goals exercise

When completing the exercise below, we strongly suggest you consider all areas of your life such as career (or work), relationships, recreational interests, personal growth, material goals and social goals. It is useful to realise how these goals interrelate and which are dependent on each other as this can affect the overall picture you build of your ideal life.

It is interesting to take a look at where you hope/expect to be in the future. This is not about writing your future in stone – it is about thinking through what you want to achieve for yourself and for those who are important to you. It helps if you do this review regularly so you can assess whether your goals need to be adjusted or changed; by looking at various key stages in your life, you may gain some perspective about what you are actually looking for and perhaps start thinking earlier how you are going to attain it.

For this exercise, we would like you to draw a circle on five pieces of paper and divide the circle into six pieces, labelled as on the diagram on page 90.

At the head of the first piece of paper, write the date and your age.

In each of the sections, write down what score you would give that aspect of your life out of 10. Next, answer the questions for each section and write down one thing you could do that would improve that score by just one.

Is your life, according to each score out of 10 and the answers you have given, a balanced one? Is that what you are aiming for?

On the second piece of paper, write down your age five years from now. Answer the questions and write down one thing you could do to improve each aspect of your life if you pushed yourself.

On the third piece of paper, write down your age in 10 years' time and follow the process above. On the fourth page, write down your age in 20 years' time and finally, on the fifth piece, your age in 30 years' time. Answer all the questions as you go in as much detail as you can. If there's not enough room in the box transfer your answers to a new piece of paper – the more detail you put down the better.

If you struggle to answer the final question about how to stretch your goals, you can leave this question blank for each section other than the first. Some people find it helpful to stretch their thinking to the future and others find it a step too far – it's a matter of going with what works for you.

Now when you review those five pages, how do you feel? Is that the life you've dreamed of? If not, what would you change? What would you improve? How have you stretched yourself?

Keep revising the pages until you have created a view of your life as you would want it to be.

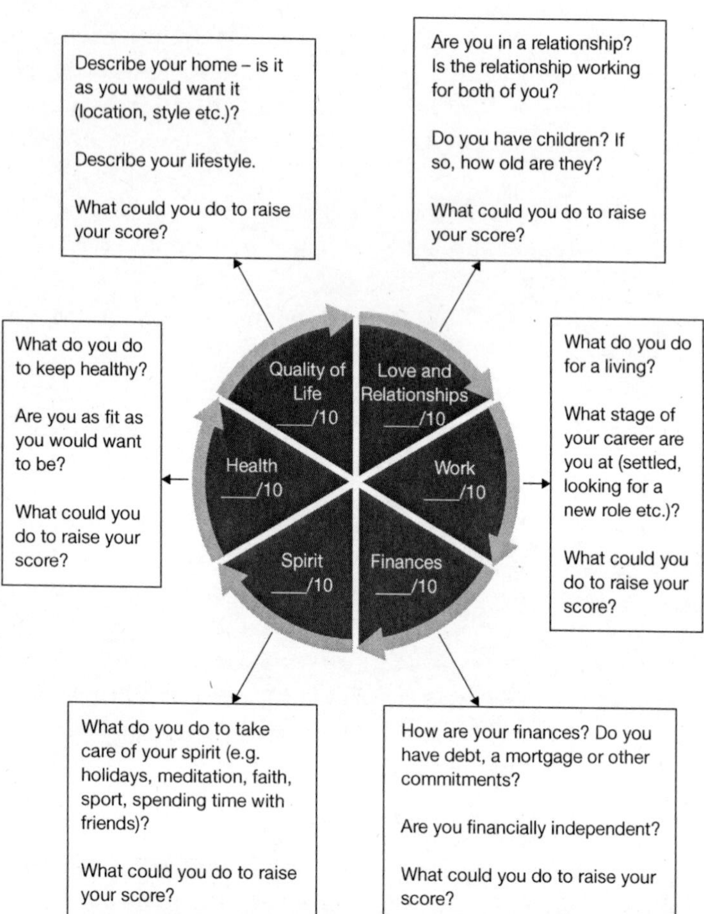

Describe your home – is it as you would want it (location, style etc.)?
Describe your lifestyle.
What could you do to raise your score?
Are you in a relationship? Is the relationship working for both of you?
Do you have children? If so, how old are they?
What could you do to raise your score?
What do you do to keep healthy?
Are you as fit as you would want to be?
What could you do to raise your score?
Quality of Life ____/10
Love and Relationships ____/10
Health ____/10
Work ____/10
Spirit ____/10
Finances ____/10
What do you do for a living?
What stage of your career are you at (settled, looking for a new role etc.)?
What could you do to raise your score?
What do you do to take care of your spirit (e.g. holidays, meditation, faith, sport, spending time with friends)?
What could you do to raise your score?
How are your finances? Do you have debt, a mortgage or other commitments?
Are you financially independent?
What could you do to raise your score?

SARAH MARSH — CASE STUDY

In my last year at school I really wanted to be a graphic designer but my parents thought that jobs in art were for people who dropped out. I was good at maths so I was persuaded to train as an accountant, which I soon realised did not need me to be good at maths! Unhappy with this career I 'dropped' into sales with a health insurer. I quite enjoyed this for about 10 years, and was good at it, but I felt limited, as if there had to be more to life. I wanted to do something that made more of a difference, that I enjoyed and which would enable me to motivate and help people.

I had always liked health and fitness so trained as a personal trainer which I enjoyed. I found it was not a particularly well paid job and I realised I had rushed into the role without thinking about its longevity, prospects etc. I started to consider retraining further in the medical/health field but did not know where to start – this was when a friend suggested I work with a career coach.

At the same time I had some difficult decisions to make personally; my husband and I needed to embark upon IVF if we were to try for a family.

I felt stuck and was going round in circles…I thought that if I was successful in starting a family I couldn't retrain – my life would be too full with caring for my child/family – and that if I didn't get pregnant could I be something different? This was where my coach was fantastic. She asked me to do two five-year plans, one with a family at the end, one without, and guess what – the result was the same. This made me feel really sure that I did want to retrain, so with help from my coach I 'tried on' various different roles: doctor, physiotherapist or osteopath.

Looking back now this seems relatively easy, but it took lots and lots of research and it needed me to look at how practically I would achieve this – costs, time involved, that sort of thing.

I decided I wanted to retrain as a physiotherapist. My nan had had a stroke and received no physiotherapy, so my decision seemed completely right. My coach helped me along the journey; she didn't do things for me, but questioned and encouraged me, helping when I felt I couldn't make it.

So over four years later I have qualified as a physiotherapist, discovered a love of yoga, completed teacher training and now combine yoga and physiotherapy for my patients.

I love my new career; I would recommend coaching to anyone. It opens your mind to options you would never have considered. It takes time, but it's realistic: it takes your commitments into consideration while helping you to see there are new opportunities out there for us all.

If you don't feel that this exercise has truly captured your future, here are a couple of others that we give to clients to help them as they develop their vision for their lives to come.

Your success article

If you are someone to whom writing comes easily, then this exercise could be the one for you.

You are going to write an article as if you are the new successful you, comfortably settled in your dream role.

What publication would you like your success profile to appear in?

What is that publication's style of writing – what would they focus the article on?

Now write the article describing how you started on your career and the steps that have been important to you to achieve success. Focus on the key stages and what it feels like to have achieved your aims; write about what you have learned that you will draw on in the future.

Your life collage

This exercise can be very useful for people who enjoy being creative (it doesn't matter whether you think you are good at being creative!).

Get a large piece of paper (preferably A0 which you can buy at most stationers) which will roll relatively easily – you will want to keep this for future reference. You will also need as large a pile of magazines as possible, scissors, glue, coloured pens and paper, a large surface to work on and preferably some time to yourself.

Flick through the magazines and rip out any pictures, words, statements, colours etc. that you are attracted to. At this stage, don't spend too much time wondering why you are attracted to them – the more images you can gather the better.

Once you have a large selection of images to choose from, start to sort them into piles. You are looking for images and words that you would like to see in your 'perfect' life. This is time to play and not become too serious. Enjoy yourself. Look at each image you have ripped out – what was it about it that attracted you? What does it represent? Is there a better image to represent that feeling, situation or person?

So if you want to live by the sea, is there an image to represent that? If you want to earn huge amounts of money, how are you going to show that? What about your hobbies? What about the people you want to have around you? Are there photos of family and friends or is there a picture to symbolise the relationship you'd like to have?

Now start to add the pictures to the large piece of paper. You can add words, colours, anything that you feel will add to the image of what you are aiming for. Look at your completed collage – have you added any pictures that give you clues to your future career direction?

Julie was still stuck about her future career direction having completed all the exercises so she made a life collage. She was working in the City and had been on a steady promotion track in financial services. Her family was proud of her as she was the first person in the family to have been to university and to have the kind of financial success she was enjoying. She, on the other hand, was depressed, angry and unsatisfied but didn't know how to change that. We were both surprised to see that her collage included no pictures of a businesswoman, money or promotion. Instead, there were pictures of beaches, children and learning, amongst others. That was the starting point of our brainstorming. What became clear was that she was in her career so as not to disappoint her family and not for herself. After much discussion, she decided to retrain as a school teacher. She has never been happier and is now working at a school where the playground faces on to a beach!

16. Putting this all together – evaluating options

Now you have done the self-assessment exercises, it's time to bring everything together. The most effective way we have found to do this and have all the information readily available in one place is by using the matrix on page 96. We have provided an example of a completed matrix on page 97.

Your aim here is to gather all the components from the assessment exercises that will comprise your perfect job. At this stage, don't exclude things that you just don't think are possible. You might like to use a spreadsheet for your matrix – one is available to download at **www.howtotakechargeofyourcareer.com**

In the matrix:

1. Choose criteria from your assessment exercises that you believe to be important in your future career. For some people it might be using their top skills, so all the skills are put in the grid. Others may decide that they only want to consider one of their interests when evaluating career options, so only one would be listed.
2. Look at your needs and make sure you cover the things that are important to you (e.g. the salary range you want to earn, your ideal location etc.).
3. Add in other preferences (such as type of environment and type of boss) if these are important to you.

There is no maximum number of items to put across the top of the matrix and we encourage people to try and come up with at least 25 items that would be components of their dream job.

Once you have filled in all the criteria that will make up your ideal job, in the possible jobs' column, list the last couple of jobs (or main jobs) you have held and then tick off how many criteria they meet in total. This gives you a review of how suitable those previous jobs have been and a benchmark against which to compare other possible options. The results can often be enlightening! For example, if you know that your previous job, which was fine but not great, gave you a score of 11 out of 25, you are definitely seeking more than 11 for the roles you are looking for.

At this stage, you may also want to highlight the criteria that are non-negotiable as far as you are concerned – this might include salary and location as there is no point in researching jobs that will ultimately not meet your needs. You may also want to weight some criteria higher than others if they are more important to you.

If you don't know whether a job or sector meets your criteria, instead of adding a tick or a cross, put in a question mark to remind you to find out the information when you come to researching at a later date.

Criteria ⇩							
TOTAL TICKS:							
POSSIBLE JOBS:							

Example:

Value: People oriented	✓	✓	?	✓
Value: Time with family	?	X	X	?
Value: Adventure	X	X	X	✓
Skills: Entrepreneurship	X	X	X	✓
Skills: Leadership	✓	X	X	✓
Skills: Strategic planning	✓	✓	?	✓
Interest: Wine	X	X	X	✓
Salary: £50k to £80k	✓	X	✓	?
Location: London	✓	✓	✓	✓
Boss must give me autonomy	?	?	?	✓
TOTAL TICKS:	**5**	**3**	**2**	**8**
POSSIBLE JOBS:	**Management consultant in small niche firm**	**Management consultant in large firm**	**Analyst**	**Set up online wine shop**

17. Brainstorming options

'An idea that is not dangerous is unworthy of being called an idea at all.'

OSCAR WILDE, Irish poet, dramatist and novelist

The final stage of Part Two is the one that our clients often find the most daunting – brainstorming options for possible jobs. They often say that their brains have gone completely blank and if they **can** come up with ideas, they dismiss them out of hand before trying them out on the matrix.

Another common question here is, 'What if I just don't know that a job exists so I narrow things down too quickly?' At some point, you are going to have to draw a line in the sand and start researching what you have come up with so far rather than prevaricating and wondering about what you don't know. Once you have decided on a sector or role, you will start the research which may well lead you to those aforementioned 'hidden' roles, so concentrate on what you know rather than what you don't.

Tom was keen to move into the wine trade but was unsure about the direction to take and had initially come up with a list of three potential roles that he could consider. One of his pieces of research to gather more 'insider language' about the industry was to find out about as many jobs in the wine trade as he could. By the time he finished, he had come up with 87 different jobs – 14 of which were distinct possibilities and two of which, when put on to the grid, were worth pursuing with more energy. He now works in the wine trade as a buyer.

Thinking laterally

This is your chance to play with ideas so don't rule anything out at this stage. If you get stuck, think as laterally as you can.

Mike had a background in the financial services industry but was keen to move out. One of his key interests was the theatre. By joining the two together, he started investigating whether it was possible to combine the two worlds and find business angels and investors for film and theatre productions.

If you are getting stuck, ask friends and family to look at the list of criteria and see whether they can come up with some ideas. Even if they are 'outside the box', their comments may spark an idea. Once you have come up with as many ideas as possible, you will see that there are perhaps three or four possibilities that have either ticked more of the criteria than any others OR that keep piquing your interest and that you want to know more about.

You should now be in a position to decide which career(s) to start investigating first. We will cover how to go about this stage in Part Three.

You may well find the matrix useful to refer back to in the future especially if you ever have to evaluate two options (perhaps two job offers). Looking again at your criteria for the perfect job may make the decision somewhat easier and help you to consider your long-term goals and what positions would work well for you in the longer term. For some clients this has meant taking a salary drop or a seemingly sideways move to gain experience to move forward.

JAMIE LUMLEY — CASE STUDY

After finishing a degree in geography I had no idea what I wanted to do for a career. I took a temporary position as an admin assistant for the NHS as an interim step. I ended up staying there for a year but I was very bored; I came to realise that working in an office was not for me but I didn't really know what I did want other than ideally working outdoors.

I went through the various exercises with Camilla and started to get a clearer picture of what I wanted; we brainstormed until I came up with a list of careers I might possibly be interested in. After some more research, it emerged that tree surgery seemed to tick all the boxes of things that I was looking for in a job.

I started a part-time course in arboriculture whilst working as a gardener. After the course I got my chainsaw and climbing certificates and found a job with a tree surgery company. I started off working as a groundsman, getting some occasional practice at climbing. Now I am a second climber, working up to becoming a full-time climber.

The biggest challenge I faced when starting off in tree surgery was being unsure whether or not I could cope with the physical aspects of the job. Getting on the job experience was very important in persuading me that I was capable of taking on the job – I wouldn't have wanted to have wasted my time and energy without knowing that. So my advice to anyone wanting to get into tree surgery or any career that would mean retraining would be to get some work experience before investing in college courses etc.

I have just finished a more advanced arboriculture course. I love the work and definitely feel I have found the right career for me. I plan to work as a tree surgeon for another five years or so when I will become a tree officer or arboriculture consultant.

It is very easy at this stage to narrow down your options too quickly and often this is because of preconceived ideas or incomplete knowledge. Ask yourself if you are dismissing an option because you know it will not work for you or because you don't have enough information to make an informed decision. Perhaps through your investigation you will find that the job you have originally identified is not for you but that, through your research, you have found an associated job that is absolutely perfect and ticks most of your criteria.

18. Optional extras – psychometric and career tests

'Genius is one per cent inspiration
and ninety-nine per cent perspiration.'
THOMAS EDISON, inventor

One area we have not yet covered is alternative ways of gathering information that may help in your decision-making process. If you have completed the exercises we have described and still feel you would like additional data, you may want to consider including the following additional information in the mix. Also, because most of the previous exercises rely on you analysing your experience, this section may be useful for people with little work experience to draw on.

We often get asked whether it is useful to take some of the career focused psychometric tests to give additional insights. Our answer may not be the one you want to hear (most people want a definitive yes or no) – it is up to you! Working on your career and deciding your career path can be hard work and many clients hope that personality questionnaires and ability tests hold the answer. Whilst they are a useful tool to help you start analysing yourself or generating ideas, they are not necessarily an end in themselves. However, for those with little experience to analyse, such as school leavers and graduates, psychometric tests can be a useful first step and provide a framework to work within.

If you have taken a test which has resonated with you then by all means factor it in to the information you are gathering. If you feel additional insight from a different direction would help with your thinking, then we have outlined below some of the options available on the market. Sadly, there is no 'crystal ball' and no one knows you better than you. It takes hard work and persistence to work on your career but it's worth it – you're worth it!

Emma Greggains, a highly experienced psychologist who has worked extensively with clients in both the private and public sectors has given us the following advice on using psychometric tests in the career development process.

Where to find psychometric tests

There is an ever increasing choice of psychometric tests available to support career development, many of them offered free on the Internet. Whilst many tests can be useful for generating ideas or looking at a specific ability or personality trait, deciding which tests are likely to be helpful for you can be a time consuming and confusing exercise.

We strongly recommend that if you are interested in taking one or more psychometric tests, that you enlist the advice and help of a professional who has been trained in the various tests available and can interpret the results; they will be able to advise which (if any) tests will add value to your career development journey. The BPS (British Psychological Society) has introduced a system of accreditation to support best practice in test use. Practitioners will hold either a 'Level A' Certificate of Competence in Occupational Testing, or the more advanced 'Level B' Certificate depending on the type of test being administered. The website **www.psychtesting.org.uk/directories** is a register held by the British Psychological Society. There is also an 'International Testing Commission' at **www.intestcom.org** which facilitates information about test use between countries. However, they do not hold a register of international test users. Specific standards and a register of test users will be provided by each country's own equivalent of the BPS, for example, there is an American Psychological Association and an Australian one etc.

The main reason why you might want to consider using psychometric test findings in your career development process is to raise your self-awareness and stimulate discussion. A skilled practitioner will facilitate your test feedback session by drawing on various sources of information, such as your existing skill set, your behavioural preferences and ability test results. A cautionary note however – a test feedback session is only a springboard for exploring different career options and should not become a distraction from the real task at hand!

Choosing the right test for you

A few words about what characterises a test in which you can have confidence. Firstly, is it reliable? In other words, are the scores produced consistent over time? And secondly, is it valid? Does the test actually measure what it says it does? Robust tests that have been rigorously researched and developed will always be supported by reliability and validity data. The British Psychological Society's Psychological Testing Centre (PTC) **www.psychtesting.org.uk**

provides a useful source of information about the services relating to standards in tests.

It is useful to think about psychometric tests as either tests of maximum performance or tests of typical performance. Each has its place in adding value to the career development process:

Tests of maximum performance

These include aptitude and ability tests and are designed to measure an individual's potential to learn. Ability test results need to be interpreted by a practitioner who holds a 'Level A' Certificate of Competence in Testing. Many ability tests developed by well-known test publishers are available online as well as in hard copy versions for ease of administration. Ability tests tend to have questions for which there is usually a right or wrong answer and a time limit.

There are a wide range of psychometrics that test how much ability individuals have in particular domains, such as abstract reasoning, numerical reasoning or verbal reasoning. Aptitude tests are also available that are specifically job related, such as tests that measure aptitude for computer programming or proofreading. In practical terms, ability tests are extremely useful for identifying what you are good at. For example, a high score on a test of numerical reasoning may open up your thinking to a wide range of different career options.

Tests of typical performance

These tend to be self-report questionnaires and broadly fall into three categories. The majority of these questionnaires will require interpretation by a practitioner who holds a 'Level B' Certificate of Competence in Testing and has been trained in the specific tool being used.

- **Personality questionnaires** assess typical or preferred ways of thinking or behaving. These do not have right or wrong answers and will usually attempt to assess how much an individual has of a particular trait, such as extroversion or perfectionism. By building up a profile of an individual's preference for behaving in certain ways, it is possible to identify career options that may (or may not) 'fit' their personality. For example, what does my preference for working in a quiet environment with opportunities to analyse people's behaviour mean for carrying out a new job role?

Numerous personality questionnaires are currently available and it is not the object of this review to list them all. However, the most robust tools are likely to be produced by the major test publishers because they have the resources to focus on extensive research and development. Usually, there is no time limit when taking a personality questionnaire.

- **Values and motivation questionnaires** are useful for assessing what is important to an individual: what drives you and what do your personal values look like? For instance, one person may report that they are motivated by a need for affiliation with other people whilst another may strongly value a role that offers material reward.

There is a comprehensive selection of well-validated values and motivation questionnaires currently available on the market. Again, you will need to enlist the support of a 'Level B' accredited practitioner with appropriate training when using one of these questionnaires as part of your career development process.

It is worth mentioning one of the most widely known bespoke career development tools, 'Career Anchors', in this section. 'Career Anchors' was developed by Edgar Schein, a leader in the field of career and professional studies and is designed to help you think about what you really want out of a career. He used the term 'Career Anchors' to describe 'patterns of self-perceived talents, motives and values which guide, constrain, stabilise and integrate the person's career'.

- **Interest inventories** assess people's preferences for particular activities. An occupational interest questionnaire will provide data

about an individual's preference for working in a particular type of job, such as nursing or engineering.

There are limited well-validated interest inventories currently available. Training is provided for certain tools, but unlike with personality and motivation questionnaires most interest inventories do not require users to have 'Level B' accreditation. Possibly the most widely known is the 'Strong Interest Inventory' which is based on Holland's six general occupational themes. 'Strong' has been used extensively for many years as part of the self-assessment stage of career planning.

As stated in the introduction to this chapter, if you feel that you need additional information to facilitate your career development review, well-chosen psychometric tests can provide you with objective and targeted data. For example, just because you are good at something does not necessarily mean that you are interested in pursuing it as part of your career! You may score highly on a numerical reasoning test but self-report feedback from an occupational personality profile might show that compared to others you are less likely to enjoy analysing data in your job. This type of feedback is extremely useful in the career development discussion and may result in one of those 'light bulb' moments that can change the focus of your thinking.

PART THREE: NOW WHAT? HOW TO RESEARCH, BRAINSTORM AND MOVE FORWARD

'Knowledge is power.'

SIR FRANCIS BACON, English author, courtier & philosopher

If you've ever read this style of book before, you may well have seen the author exhorting you to go through each stage one at a time and to follow the process from beginning to end. Over the years, we have both read countless of these books for our own development, research and interest. We have done what the majority of people do, flick through the book and think, I'll get back to doing the exercises when I get a moment. It was only when we started putting this book together that we suddenly understood the pleas of those other authors. We know, through years of practice, that this methodology can really work if you just go through each phase systematically. If we were with you in person, coaching you through this process, we would be there to spot those moments of doubt written on your face or to deal with the 'Yes buts…' that inevitably follow. We hope that you will be determined enough to do this for yourself. If you have side-tracked the exercises so far or have missed out one or two that you don't feel you want to do, you should go back now and complete them, and start this new section with a renewed vigour and belief that you really can work towards your career goal.

If we are not giving you the benefit of the doubt and you have followed the book – we apologise! If you have completed Part Two, you will now have a sense of your key skills and experience, you will have a good idea of what you are looking for in your ideal job and you will have brainstormed some ideas of careers to research. We also hope you have overcome any obstacles that are standing in your path or have a plan for how to cope with them when, or if they appear.

Part Three covers how you narrow down your brainstormed ideas into tangible options. We will look at how you deal with the world of work when it doesn't seem to fit with your life circumstances either in the short or long term and how to create an action plan. Finally, in Part Four, we will review best practice in the art of job applications and negotiation.

The start to this section can appear daunting to some as most of the work to date can be done below the radar – you can look at yourself and potential options without necessarily sharing what you are doing with other people. Now you will have to venture out into the open and that can be a nerve-wracking time for many, especially those who are naturally introverted. Now, more than ever, having a positive support network around you to spur you on can help enormously. You may occasionally find your heart in your mouth as you make some research calls or start networking. Given that the research piece is a crucial element of the process and incredibly useful we hope you will work your way through any residual fear with the end goal of finding the right job clearly in your sights.

19. Researching – separating perception from reality

As we have mentioned several times in the book so far, the more real information/data you have, the easier it is going to be to make a decision about whether a career or company is the right one for you. We so often lose sight of what reality and perception actually are so systematic research from a variety of different sources will help immeasurably as you start to narrow down your brainstormed options to a clear favourite to which you can apply all your energies.

For many clients this stage takes months. The length of this phase is driven by whether you are working or not and how much time you can dedicate to it.

Finding time for research

How long it will take you will depend on the priority you assign to your research and the clear, measurable goals you have set in this area. As we know, occasionally life can get in the way of the best laid plans. We know from experience that it is very easy to let this phase drift and you can lose track of what you are trying to find out and why. The more time you can find from your already busy life, the faster you will complete this part of the process. We know that if you have a full-time job or children, time will be at a premium, but time you devote to this process will be useful – even the odd snatched five minutes of research on the Internet still gets you closer to your goal. Many people want to move through this phase as quickly as possible in order to get closer to their end goal but the time you spend doing this research in depth will pay dividends in the long run. Go at the right pace for you – just maintain momentum and do it little and often rather than putting it to one side and swearing to yourself that you'll get back to it another time. Another time rarely comes…

Maintaining your career folder

As you go through this research stage, it is very important to review your matrix. It is your touchstone – after every piece of research you will need to 'check in' and evaluate what you have found alongside what you have identified as important to you and what you want to achieve. Some options will be ceremoniously struck off the list. This is a positive step as you can then focus more of your time and energy on the other areas you want to investigate that are still viable options.

As you gather information from your research, add it to your career folder so that you know where everything is rather than having to start from scratch each time. For example, if you are on the Internet and see a press release from a company that is in the sector you are potentially interested in but you are running out the door to an appointment, print it off, put it in your career folder and read it when you have a moment. Sod's Law says that if you think you'll look up the site and article again when you get back, you will either forget all about it or won't be able to find it. Also, if you keep all the information in one place, when you have a meeting with someone from the sector or company, you can easily find all the references you have come across to review before the meeting, saving time.

Your matrix is your starting point to highlighting what information you need to find out; it tells you about the sector you are interested in, the function you would like to know more about or to ask more specific questions to ascertain whether, for example, a potential career will pay you the salary you are looking for or will match up with a particular value or skill you have identified as important.

Once you have identified what you need to know, the next stage is to work out how best to find that information. Your starting point is the Internet, a great resource for gathering information. Think of every possible route to find out what you are looking for and follow each link to a new site, until you feel you have exhausted all your options. If you do not have access to a computer, try your local library. They will often have computers you can access but they often also stock copies of periodicals from major industry sectors which may give you new information.

Once you have gathered all the data you can from these sources, you will be left with a list of things you need to know that are best obtained from people who work in that field.

Different types of research

1. Passive information gathering

This is probably the most obvious form of research but one worth mentioning all the same. So far, you have a list of potential sectors or even potential roles that you might be interested in. If it is a sector or job you are already familiar with, you will be supplementing the information you already have. If, however, these are completely new sectors to you, then you are about to go on a fascinating voyage of discovery into a new world. OK, perhaps that's a little grand but before you get started on the research, you need to be in the right frame of mind to hunt out all the vital details you need to make a very important decision – one that might affect a good deal of your happiness and sense of fulfilment in the workplace. Over the years, we have found that many of our clients have tried to cut short this part and feel that a cursory look at a sector will tell them all they need to know.

That may well stand you in good stead to make primary decisions based on factors such as the career will not pay you the salary you require or will require high fitness levels which is not you at all.

However, if a sector or career starts to look like it might well be a possibility, the more in-depth information you gather, the better off you will be. This is for a few reasons:

- It will allow you to make an informed decision about whether it matches with what you are looking for.
- You will start to get a greater insight into the industry.
- You will start to inadvertently gather 'insider language' which will help in future information gathering with individuals involved in the industry and you'll come across more impressively at interviews.

'Insider language'

If you think of anything you have a certain amount of knowledge about (your favourite musician, hobby, club, city), you will recognise that there are certain words and phrases that only someone who is similarly knowledgeable will know. You may recall being at a social engagement where there's lots of noise; you are deep in conversation with someone but then you hear someone else in a different group, a group you haven't been listening to, mention something that resonates with you, like the name of an obscure artist whose show you have just seen. We instantly look for similarity in people and that sort of reference gives us an immediate connection. We recognise someone who is probably like-minded – you are insiders. On the other hand, we've all come across people who have ended up looking foolish when they pretend to be what they're not and dig themselves into a hole. The same is true when you express an interest in a sector or career. The more information you have or the more 'insider language' that you hear, assimilate and start using naturally, the more likely you are to be accepted as one of the 'in-crowd' and you'll have created a bond. As with most people, we are more likely to be well-disposed and helpful to those who are on the same wavelength as us or who talk the same language.

So the upshot of all that is that the more information you uncover, however insignificant it might seem, the better – it may just give you the edge in future conversations with people who are able to help you in your job search. And anything that can you give an edge is worth having!

General information

The starting point (if you don't already have it) is generalist sector information. This is the foundation to any future research and may well give you vital details that can count as an option from your matrix.

How broad is the sector? Are there many different aspects to it (e.g. banking can be narrowed down to a list that includes investment banking, retail banking, private banking and so on). Can you narrow down which part of the sector would interest you? Questions to consider include:

- What are the main organisations in that sector?
- How is the sector doing in the economic climate – is it on the rise or in decline?
- Have any books been written about the sector as a whole?
- What are the main periodicals written for that sector and how can you access them?
- Does the sector hold conferences that are open to the public – if so, where and when?
- Who are the main commentators on the sector (journalists, experts etc.)?
- Is there a governing body for the sector?

Again, the Internet is a great place to start with this kind of research. First, put the sector into a search engine and see what comes up – is it a company name? Does it have a Wikipedia entry? Once you have exhausted the information from this preliminary search, work through each of the questions above using the search engine.

Make a note of key websites or names that keep coming up that may be useful as you progress.

As you work through this research, ask yourself whether it is making things any clearer for you. It may seem obvious but it is easy to get caught up in gathering information and then losing sight of why you're gathering it. Are you starting to see a particular part of the sector that appeals to you more than any other? What is it about that part of the sector that is interesting you? Is this sector still looking like a good option for you? If you don't know the answer, what else do you need to know about the sector to decide whether it is a good option?

Keep going until you have a sense of whether the sector is the one for you. Once you have enough information to decide whether, say, the financial services sector appeals to you, can you narrow the sector down further into a specific area of the this sector? If, in your research, you have decided that private banking is the place you would like to concentrate further investigation, you can then refine the search for information. You may find that you still have more than one sector that piques your interest so try and narrow each sector down to one particular area of focus with the information you have gathered.

We have given you a list of information that will prove useful but don't stop there – what else, on a general level, could you add to your research?

More detailed information

Look at what you have already gathered on the particular area that you are now going to focus on. What information do you still need? To get you started, here are some ideas for gathering more detailed information:

1. Put together a list of all the roles you can find in the industry you are interested in – make the list as exhaustive as possible (remember Tom who managed to come up with 87 options in the wine trade).
2. Delete any of these roles that do not appeal at all.
3. Find out what qualifications or entry requirements are needed for each of the roles.
4. Who are the main employers in this industry – do their websites have additional information that would prove useful? Do they advertise potential roles on their websites?
5. Gather more detailed information from magazines and trade

association websites, paying particular attention to any articles that draw your eye – what aspects of these articles interested you? Could that give you additional information or suggest this is an avenue to investigate more?

6. Start putting together a list of key protagonists in the industry – are there lecturers on the industry, journalists or key industry people who have been profiled? Can you find out how to get in touch with those people either by phone or by email?

As you gather more information, some of it will lead you to want to develop new lines of investigation and some will make it clear that a direction is not for you. Each time that you add a new line of enquiry or shut one down, it is progress, even if it doesn't always feel that way.

Since Caroline was a child, she had always had an interest in accident investigation but when she had mentioned this to her family, they had joked with her about it, telling her it was far too gruesome a profession for her. She had taken that at face value and so had never pursued it as a possible career. When she started her coaching, she talked about how she was still intrigued about accident investigation and kept coming back to it as an option. Her first piece of research was to find out all the different kinds of roles within accident investigation and their entry requirements. She discovered that you needed to go through the police to train in accident investigation so arranged a meeting at the police's local recruitment centre to discuss how she might get into the field. They were extremely helpful – they told her that she would need to train as a police officer and then after a certain amount of time, she could apply to train in accident investigation but that there were no guarantees. She spoke to a couple of people in the field and did a little further investigation but what became clear was that she was not interested in a career with the police without a guarantee that she would end up in the discipline of her choice. Her research also gave her enough information for her to realise that the career was not for her – not because it was too gruesome but for family circumstances. As soon as she had shut this down as a possibility, she was able to focus more on what felt right for her. She is now in her chosen field of sales and marketing.

Often we find our clients have to cross things off the list in order to move forward. This act of finally dismissing a career avenue can be tremendously liberating because an option that had been floating around in your head can either move to being a serious contender for your future career or removed as an option once and for all.

Return to the matrix. Has the information you have gathered so far answered any of the question marks you had in place? Have you deleted any of your brainstorm options because of your research? Have you added any new options to the matrix and marked it up against your criteria?

2. Active information gathering: networking

As you will see from Caroline's story, once she had done all the information gathering she could from passive sources, the next step was to start talking to people in the field she wanted to know more about.

When networking is mentioned it usually conjures up images of rooms full of people you don't know who you have to approach to get their contact details or to give them yours – a hugely stressful thought for most people, even some extroverts!

We help people we know, like and trust and that is your jumping off point. It is so easy to overlook the people closest to you as a source of help and assistance: it is very important you tell your friends and family that you are researching certain jobs or fields. It is highly likely you don't know all their network and you certainly don't know who they are going to sit next to on a train or talk to at a party – they need to be your eyes and ears. Many people have someone in the family or a friend who is always sending newspaper clippings or chatting to anyone and everyone – recruit them to your exploration team.

Now it's your turn to start networking and gathering information from the people who are in the know. There's no getting away from it – this is the part that most people find the most daunting. Picking up the phone to talk to someone to ask for help can be nerve-wracking, particularly if you don't know them or the link to them is tenuous at best. However, at this stage, it's a crucial part of the process as you are still likely to have many questions about what is required for a particular position in the industry of your choice.

We have worked with hundreds of people who have faced this stage with trepidation and so we have tried to lay out some tried and tested routes to getting the information you need in as painless a way as possible. Clearly, adapt these thoughts so that they work for you and the person you are approaching but we hope that it will give you a good starting point.

First steps

As you have been gathering your information, hopefully you will have started to note some names of key individuals who might be useful for you to meet. Do you have their contact information? If not, that's the first step. If you know where they work, perhaps the company's website can give you their contact details or at the least, a main switchboard number. We will return to this group of individuals in due course but making a 'cold call', i.e. a call to someone who you don't know and who has no reason to take your call can be the most scary so let's look at how you can gather some 'warmer' options – those people where there might be some form of connection in place already.

You may have heard of the concept of the 'six degrees of separation'. It was an idea that was developed in a play, and later a film, written by John Guare that looks at the idea that you are one link away from each person you know, and then two links away from each person that each of those individuals knows and so on to a point where we are only six links away from every individual on earth. There are several networking sites that work on this basis – our favourite for business networking being LinkedIn (**www.linkedin.com**) which can help you connect through your network to someone else.

You may shrug your shoulders and say that it won't work for you but we think you'll be surprised if you approach this portion of research with an open mind.

Your first step is to start telling those people who are one link away from you that you are trying to meet people who are involved in a particular job or industry and ask if they know anyone they could introduce you to. Start with the easy ones – your family and closest friends – and then gradually widen the network of people you ask. You will be surprised who people manage to come up with – and don't discount asking anyone. Your cousin the farmer may not be the most obvious person to ask if they know anyone in sport management but perhaps they were at school with someone whose partner works in the field. Never presume you know who can help – ask!

One of the things to keep in mind as you do this is that people love to help especially if it makes them seem knowledgeable/an expert in the process. If one of your family or friends approached you to help you find individuals in your chosen field, would you offer to help? We are hoping you would! Work on the basis that the people you are going to approach feel the same way.

KAYE KENT CASE STUDY

My best subject has always been art. However, there wasn't very good career advice available at my school and I ended up drifting into art college and then a history of art degree. Still unsure what I wanted to do after graduating, I went on to complete a heritage studies MA, to train as a curator.

After getting my first professional job in a gallery on the south coast, I realised that working in the public sector wasn't for me, so I tried various jobs in commercial galleries, which suited me better. However, I always had to go where the work was and ended up moving to new places around the country several times. I finally got my big break working as an art consultant for a company in Liverpool – and it really was my dream job! I had to create a range of art from scratch to suit interior design projects, which involved travelling all over the UK, looking at art and meeting artists. Heaven! The problem was, I had found a job I loved, but it was located in the wrong place as I desperately wanted to move back home to Yorkshire.

Finally, push came to shove and I decided for the first time to put my personal life before work, so I took the plunge and relocated. I tried to continue with my job from home for a while, but I felt very isolated and missed being in a busy working environment. With so few other opportunities around, I realised a career change was my only option.

I had always been interested in the idea of working in TV, but had no idea where to start. It was though a friend who is a cameraman that I was advised to try and get some work experience at Yorkshire TV. I was accepted on a two-week placement in the art department, during which I got my first insight into this world. With luck, a new period drama was going into production as my placement finished, and I was taken on as the art department runner – a great opportunity to work on an actual production.

Since then, I have worked on several TV dramas, and I am now working towards a career as a Production Buyer/Set Decorator. This ties in with my period knowledge, an eye for interior design, creativity and versatility, which always keeps my working life varied and challenging. The hours are long and the lack of job security as a freelancer can be stressful – but I have finally found my true vocation and I am so happy I had the courage to make a change.

Top tips

If someone gives you a lead, follow it up – there's nothing worse than helping someone out who does nothing about it. Thank them for their help and then let them know how the contact has worked out – the vast majority of people like to help but they also like to be thanked!

If they do have a lead that you can follow up on, ask if they would be prepared to make the introduction rather than just giving you the contact details. If they are, ask if they would find out if the person they are recommending you to would mind you calling to arrange a meeting or having a 20 minute phone call so that you can ask them questions about their field. Make it clear that you are not looking for a job at this stage, just information.

Your career database

Keep a record of everyone you come across and their contact details – you never know when you might need to get back in touch so it is useful to keep their information in one place. We would suggest either a small database or perhaps a spreadsheet such as the one below:

First name	Last name	Introducer	Email	Contact numbers	Company	Last contact	Status
John	Gordon	Kay Williams	johngordon@hotmail.com			Dec 2010	Mentioned he would introduce me to colleague James Wills

This will give you a running overview of progress you're making and will ensure you follow up on potential new leads. Additionally you won't have to rely on your memory as to where you put their business card or when they asked you to call back if they were unable to speak when you first called.

Prepare your approach

Before you start making calls to the people you have been introduced to, it is worth making a list of the information you want to gain from the conversation. Questions you might want to consider asking include:

1. How did you get into working in this field? What was your background?
2. What do you like most/least about what you do and this industry?

3. When you are recruiting someone, what skills and qualifications do you look for?
4. If you were in my position, looking to get into this career, what would you do next?
5. When you are recruiting, how do you go about it? Do you recruit through an agency, advertise on your website or in a particular publication? (This will give you a new lead on how best to apply for roles if you decide you want to go forward).
6. Is there anything else you think it would be useful for me to know that I haven't asked? (This is a very generic question but can often yield some fascinating information!).
7. Is there anyone else you could introduce me to who could help in my search for information before I decide to pursue a career in the field?

Clearly you will want to add in your own questions, particularly targeting information that you need in order to answer any remaining questions you have from your matrix. You may also want to ask if they would mind you contacting them again if you have further questions.

Making contact

Once you have your list of questions prepared, now is the time to pick up the phone or draft an email asking for help, whichever way your contact has suggested you get in touch. When you get in contact, mention your mutual acquaintance and the fact they had helped with the introduction. Ask if it would be possible to take 20 minutes of their time, either in person or over the phone, to ask them a few questions about their field – again, reiterate that **you are not looking for a job at this stage**; it is just information gathering. Most people are curious as to why you would mention that you're not looking for a job when it is highly likely you will be. The reason for this is that while most people are very happy to be helpful with information, they are usually more reticent about being put in a position where they may have to disappoint you by saying no, there is no job – they will therefore avoid a situation where that might arise. If you take that possibility out of the equation as you start your conversation, they will often relax and be even happier to help out. Don't presume that if you have got straight through to them, that they are available instantly to start answering your questions – they may prefer to schedule a time that is more convenient so it is worth asking what would work best for them.

Once you have started your information gathering interview with them and have had the OK that the time is convenient, it is up to you to manage the interview time – if you've asked for 20 minutes, stick to 20 minutes. If you are running out of time, mention that you recognise you asked for 20 minutes but you have a few quick questions to ask, and would that be OK? The person you are talking to will appreciate your consideration and will usually give you the extra time you need.

When you are meeting face-to-face, if you want to take notes, it is worth asking whether the person you are talking to is comfortable with that. Again, most people appreciate the question and will have no problem with it.

Consolidate your information

Once your call or meeting is over, find yourself somewhere quiet to sit down and write down any additional information you want to capture including the contact information from anyone else they've suggested you talk to. It's so tempting to think you will remember what has been said or that you'll do it later, but it is amazing how useful gems of information can be lost by the following day.

Keep revising the questions you ask to take into account the information you have gathered at each meeting. If you now have a picture of the qualifications you need for the role you have identified, you don't need to keep asking that same question but you may want to ask their opinion on the best place to train. As you gain more information, so your questions will become more focused and will reference 'insider language' which will help to develop a greater rapport at this information gathering stage but will also prove vital when you are interviewing for specific roles.

Once you have met or spoken to all the contacts that have resulted from your immediate circle of friends with direct introductions, you will want to contact the people whose contact details you have but no one to introduce you. Welcome to the world of networking!

The contact is very similar to that outlined above but if you don't know anyone in common, then reference how you have come across their name (perhaps they spoke at a conference or wrote an article that you particularly liked) and ask whether it would be possible for you to have just 20 minutes of their time. You are more likely to get negative responses to these approaches than to the approaches where you had a direct introduction as there is no compunction to help you. Don't become down-hearted if you are told they can't help – it's just part of the process. It is always worth asking whether they can recommend anyone else who might be able to help in your information gathering – you never know, you might get a new contact. And it is far easier to call up a potential lead saying that you have been given their name by someone who is well-known in an industry! Anything that helps is worth pursuing.

As you conclude this phase of your research, have you answered all the questions that were showing up as question marks on your matrix? Have you started to focus on one particular career option? If there are still some gaps missing in your knowledge, who can help you get the information you need?

You may feel that what we are about to say next is common sense and just being polite but it is amazing how many people don't think about the social niceties of gathering information so we apologise if we offend those of you who would take this as a matter of course; it's just a suggestion...Say thank you to the person you have interviewed for information! It seems simple but it is often overlooked.

Next steps in networking

You may now have followed up everyone you can possibly think of or you've stalled and want a new approach to keep your enthusiasm going. At this point, you might want to consider stepping into the lion's den and attending either a networking meeting that is designed for like-minded individuals to meet. Try putting networking, your chosen industry and your location into a search engine and see what comes up.

Most professions have an affiliated association and this can be a good starting point. Initially you may go along to conferences and exhibitions to find out more about this field, get attendee lists and see what the burning issues are. If you are doing further study as a mechanism to change career, you might use conferences as a way to help you decide the focus of your project or dissertation.

Many of the successful MBA students that Jane works with use their project strategically as a way to get experience in a new field or industry. They choose a subject which is very topical and one that can be shared or partly shared with other companies in that field so they have something to offer other organisations if they don't get hired by the company where they are doing their project. The company they choose to do their project with often introduces them to suppliers and partners who can be useful contacts at the end of the MBA. The least successful students often just take a project offered by the business school in an area unrelated to their long-term career goals.

KLAUDIUSZ ZWOLINSKI CASE STUDY

After graduating from a technical university in Poland, I moved first to Germany and then to Belgium to work for an international logistics integrator. I worked in the European headquarters in several functions across marketing and sales. The work was great, with challenging projects, and I worked in an international, experienced and supportive team.

After a few years, I started wondering if logistics was really the industry in which I wanted to work for the next 30 years. I realised that I was more interested in the financial sector and so I decided to apply for an MBA to extend my knowledge, develop new skills and instigate a career change. The programme was a highly stimulating experience and enabled me to move in the direction I wanted. However, it was not easy.

With no specific financial studies and a professional background in logistics, it was difficult to make the switch. The approaching financial crisis made the situation even more challenging. Nevertheless, I was persistent. An MBA project in a respected venture capital fund helped me to gain valuable insights and build credibility. I now work as an in-house management consultant in a multinational financial institution. The work is exciting and I feel pleased about the change I made.

My advice to anyone is to constantly look for what you truly enjoy doing. Once you collect more experience, the picture becomes clearer but the shift is more difficult as well. An MBA or advice from a professional career coach is a very good way to put you back on the right track.

Attending a networking meeting may be a step too far for some people but we would encourage you to try if you can. If you can't, then so be it – there must be another way to get an introduction or the information you're looking for – it will just take a little ingenuity!

It is always worth bearing in mind that master networker Thomas Power of the e-networking site Ecademy (**www.ecademy.com**) works on a metric of 49/1 i.e. out of 49 people he meets, he expects to gain one referral. Don't set yourself unrealistic targets when you start networking!

When you are career hunting you are never off duty!

When you are working your way through this book, it is always useful to consider yourself continually on the hunt for information. You never know where the vital piece of information or lead will come from that will be the final jigsaw piece that helps you make the move into a new career or role. Again it's a case of telling people what you are looking for so they can help you if the opportunity arises.

LAURA BEVILL CASE STUDY

Prior to my MBA, I was a management consultant. I did my summer project at Lloyds TSB which I had found by speaking to an Exec MBA who I met through the MBA programme at University of Bath, School of Management. My mentor was someone I had met through church in Boston, USA. His former boss happened to be working with an intermediary who had a relationship with a global investment solutions firm which had recently won some new business. My mentor's former boss asked him if he knew someone who might be suitable for a new role that had opened up. My mentor recommended me and a global investment solutions firm saw my experience with Lloyds TSB as having given me valuable insights into their new client and made me an offer.

Remember, if you don't ask for help, you won't get it! Stretch yourself and use your powers of deduction to find all the information and contacts you need to decide whether you are ready to move in that direction.

Mentors can be found in unusual places; Amit Pandey found his on the cricket field which led to him securing a Business Project Manager role at a world-leading financial services firm. This was particularly impressive as he was a foreign student studying for his MBA at Leeds University Business School with no significant network in the UK.

Common concerns

Over the years, we have come across some concerns about this aspect of information gathering so we thought it would be useful to tell you what they are and our usual responses to them – you are not alone but sadly we're also not letting you off the hook!

What if that person doesn't want to see me?

It may happen, and if it does just move on! That's life.

Why would they help me?

Change your mindset. Contact them with the anticipation that they will help you. We find that most of the time, people do want to help if they are approached with courtesy and consideration. If they don't, it's a numbers game, just move on to the next contact. If, however, this keeps happening then you should ask for feedback as to whether your approach or communication style could be improved.

Won't they think I work for the competition and will therefore be reluctant to share information?

Most people are confident in their own ability and happy to share with others just starting out. However, if you are thinking, for example, of setting up a florist shop in your home town, it would probably not make sense to do informational interviews with other florists in the same area because they are likely to feel threatened and won't want to share their trade secrets! Instead you could approach florists in towns, say, 100 miles away.

I am nervous and feel shy

Most people feel nervous when they start this part of the information gathering process; it is a case of finding a way to work through it. Perhaps you've never interviewed people before and want to practise that before you start speaking to people in your chosen career. If so, have some fun interviewing friends about their jobs, regardless of whether they're relevant to what you want to do. It is about finding your confidence that you *can* interview and get the information you need in a safe place. This will build your confidence to move to the next phase.

How do I find people to interview?

Start with people who know you well because they are more likely to help. Family, extended family, school friends, university friends, friends connected with your hobbies or sport, church contacts or people you meet at networking events all count. Tell them you are looking for contacts in these fields and ask if they know anyone who might be open to talking to you.

No one close to me knows anyone in this field

Then you need to start contacting people direct. Refer back to the publications and conferences you've already sourced for names of people to contact. Now is your opportunity to start networking.

What happens if they say that they think they might have a job for me when I've already said this isn't about a job search?

Smile and say you'd be delighted to know more about the potential role. It depends on where you are in your information gathering as to whether you know if you are definitely interested in this career. You can explain why you said initially that you weren't looking for a role, just information. **However,** don't leap at the first job you hear about or are offered – the whole point of this book is to find the right fit for you, not just any job in your chosen field, so it is fine to express an interest in knowing more but continue with your due diligence as you proceed.

I still don't know where I'm heading – what should I do?

We would love to tell you that you will immediately discover the right career for you but it doesn't always work out that way. What we do know is that we have not met anyone who has maintained the momentum and the resolve but who has not ultimately come up with a solution that works for them. If you are struggling, then this is what we would advise you to do:

I have no idea about what I have to offer – go back to the exercises in Part Two.

I have no idea about what I want to do – go back to the matrix in Chapter 16 Part Two.

I am confused; there are too many options – use the matrix to structure your research and evaluate your options against them. You should find you are crossing some off!

I don't have enough options – brainstorm with friends or a career coach.

I don't know what jobs out there would suit me – you need to do more research.

I don't know what industry to go into – go back to the interests exercise in Chapter 11.

What next?

Once you have done as much research as you feel you need to give you a clear direction, you can then move forward to the next stage. Following the research you have done, have you decided on just one option? If not, what else do you need to know to make a decision? You may need to do more research, perhaps talk to more people or go back to the brainstorming stage if you are still not sure.

Once you have narrowed down your options to one that feels right, you can then start to build a strategy for the next steps.

The first thing to assess is what is standing in your way of making progress towards getting the role you want. Amongst the things you might need to consider are:

- Do you have the financial resources to make a change?
- Do you need to retrain to move in your new direction? If so, can you support yourself while you retrain?
- Do you still have some residual questions about what it would be like to work in the field? Would they be answered by further research or interviewing? Perhaps you could volunteer with an organisation in the field to get hands-on experience.

We encourage you to keep gathering information until you have enough to convince you that the change you are looking at makes sense. Change of any kind is always difficult and much has been written about the subject. There comes a time for everyone who is looking to make a change in their careers to take a leap of faith. At that point it is time for action.

If you don't take this next step and keep the momentum going, your career folder will be full of what could have been if you had just taken the next step rather than staying put and wondering what it would have been like to have found the right job for you.

20. Creating an action plan

'A goal without a plan is just a wish.'
ANTOINE DE SAINT-EXUPÉRY, French writer and aviator

The next steps you have to take will be uniquely your own. The common ones we often hear about are:

- talking to people who would be affected by your change in direction;
- building up a financial reserve or downsizing so it is possible to make a move;
- finding out about retraining and qualifications;
- arranging to go part time in your current role as you gain experience in your new field;
- rewriting your CV in line with your new goals (see Part Four for guidance on how to do this effectively);
- creating a timeline for a potential career – what is the starting point and what are the promotion prospects?

One of the hardest things once you have decided you want to actively take charge of your career is to keep the momentum going. You have come a long way – don't give up now! Make a list of all the actions you need to carry out and create a timeline of when you will achieve them by. For example:

To do	How	By when	Reward
Redo my CV	Refer to Part Four and then get a friend to check for mistakes	End of the month	Watch a new DVD
Contact 100 target companies	Research on Internet and use LinkedIn to find the right person to contact	In next two months	Go out for dinner

We have put in a reward as it's important to stay motivated and for some people incentives can help. Sometimes the actual day when you start doing what you have always dreamed of feels a long way off and you need to keep motivated as you work towards it.

If you are trying to get a sense of how long you will need to commit to this, it can also help to draw up a reverse timeline. This will help you stay on track and possibly change your expectations as to how long things will actually take to achieve (e.g. if you do have to retrain).

Reverse timeline

Take a blank piece of paper and turn it sideways. Create a flow chart across the page halfway down. Write your goal in the box to the far right of the page and establish your ideal date to achieve that goal. Then work your way back from the right to the left of the page in three-month increments, writing down what you will have to have achieved by that point in order to complete your goal – keep working your way back until you have all the action points listed. Does it take you back to today? If not, does that mean you will realistically need to make more time to achieve the goal or could you shorten the time frame?

Reverse timeline example:

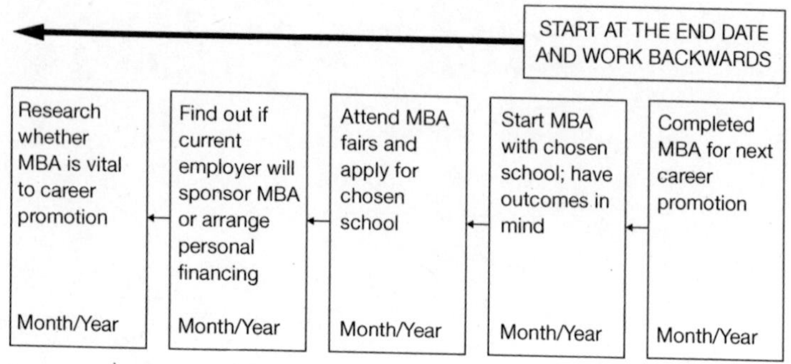
START AT THE END DATE AND WORK BACKWARDS
Research whether MBA is vital to career promotion
Month/Year
Find out if current employer will sponsor MBA or arrange personal financing
Month/Year
Attend MBA fairs and apply for chosen school
Month/Year
Start MBA with chosen school; have outcomes in mind
Month/Year
Completed MBA for next career promotion
Month/Year

When you have decided on a goal, the next step is to plan how you will achieve it. Stephen R. Covey says it best: 'Begin with the end in mind'.

21. Returning to work

'Life shrinks or expands in proportion to one's courage.'
ANAÏS NIN, French author

Returning to the workplace – whatever the reason you have taken some time out – can be a daunting prospect. Our experience of working with many people in this situation over the years is that the perception of the issues that are facing them is often the biggest hurdle they have to overcome. When we sit down and talk through all the problems they anticipate as they try to find a new job, the list can seem endless or insurmountable. We promise that it's not – we just need to work out what is perception and what is reality and then start working out how to defeat each and every issue. You will face difficulties, there's no getting around that, and there's no point pretending otherwise but as the quote goes, 'If you think you can, or you think you can't, you're right.' We have seen so many people defeat what looked like insurmountable odds to finding a great role for them that we have faith you can do the same.

Fear and lack of confidence can be the biggest hurdles facing those returning to work after a break. Whether you have taken time out of your career to parent your children, continue your education, take a sabbatical or whether you were made redundant and haven't found a job yet, the sense of being removed from the working world and that it has moved on without you (whilst also leaving a gap on your CV) can keep many people from moving forward with their search.

The exercises that we have run through so far apply to you regardless of your age, education or personal circumstances. You may have additional needs in terms of what you are looking for in your matrix – perhaps you need disabled access to the building where you work or need to take school holidays off work or require flexibility in terms of your hours. Whatever your needs are, it may take you longer to find the employer for you, but if you are a compelling candidate who is hard-working and passionate, you will find someone who will recognise your talents and will work with you to accommodate your needs. We strongly suggest that this is your starting point.

Perceived obstacles

One of the biggest pitfalls we find when we are working with people who have been out of work for a while (when we talk about work, we are talking about the workplace rather than insinuating that anything you have been doing in the meantime hasn't been work!) is that they get in their own way when it comes to finding a job. Rather than sitting down and working out the skills they have added to their list, they focus on the skills that are outdated. At interviews, they will often spend time pointing out that they haven't worked for a while rather than highlighting what they can do for the employer and how their skill set matches with skills listed in the job specification.

It is important that you focus on the positive, whilst acknowledging any potential concerns from a future employer. If they ask why you haven't worked for five years, don't become defensive; give a succinct, clear answer that explains why you have been out of the workplace and why you are now so keen on returning in general and to this job in particular. If, for example, you are asked about how you will deal with childcare, again be succinct and to the point to give reassurance to the interviewer that you are in control and it will not be a concern for them. Most interviewers are just trying to find the best person for the job and they want you to tell them why that person is you.

Support networks

If you know several people who are in a similar position, why not set up a support network? We recently worked with a group of stay-at-home mothers who were all considering how they could start earning some money now that their children had started school. They all had different needs in terms of how much they wanted to earn and how much time they could work depending on their childcare arrangements but their fears were pretty similar. 'I haven't worked for ages, I've forgotten what I can do', 'There are younger versions of me who can do what I do, why would someone hire me?', 'Technology has moved on in the five years since I last set foot in an office' – you could probably continue with the list yourself. This particular group asked us to come and talk them through the exercises which they all completed and then we facilitated an initial get-together one morning to give them each a starting point with an action plan for research and exploration, building upon their matrix. They then continued to meet fortnightly, chatting between meetings if they needed help, to keep their momentum going. Three months after starting their group, two had decided to start a business from home, one trained as a virtual assistant working from home and one is hoping to retrain as a teacher.

Can you find a group like this in your area? Could you start one with some like-minded people? If you would prefer to work one-to-one with someone, perhaps you can complete the matrix and then look at hiring a coach to get you past your fears and lack of confidence.

22. Retirees and 'third age' workers

'Do not regret growing older.
It is a privilege denied to many.'
Author unknown

As we are an ageing population more people are considering working past the official retirement age. This book works whatever your age and circumstances and we encourage you, if you are in your 'third age', to look at all opportunities and consider potential new horizons rather than sticking with what you've always done.

Ageism

There's no getting away from it – ageism exists and unfortunately there will be some companies or clients who discriminate against you in terms of age at either end of the spectrum but there are plenty who won't and who see experience as an advantage. Often it's a numbers game to find the employers who are more open minded. We have seen many examples of people who have found work later in life but we have also seen employers who unconsciously deter would-be employees.

If you feel being older is an issue, consider the following:

- How can you keep young? While we are not suggesting you suddenly don the latest fashions, outdated clothes can age you. Ask someone you admire for the way they dress for some help or engage the services of an image consultant.
- What are your energy levels like? Do you look enthusiastic and motivated? Be honest with yourself. Doing work you enjoy goes a long way to helping with this and hence it's important to follow the exercises in the book.
- How can you put a positive spin on your extensive experience? What mistakes have you seen that you could help other people avoid? What solutions could you suggest based on your experience?

- Keep up to date with technology. Whether you like it or not technology is here to stay and in many work environments, it's important that you embrace it if you want to stay employable. There are many different ways of learning about technology either at local colleges of education or from individual tutors if you prefer.
- Double check your own attitude to ageism. Are you *expecting* to come across it when you approach someone for a job? Are you *presuming* that you will be counted out at interview stage if you are a little older? If so, deal with those limiting beliefs before you start looking for a new job.
- Lack of experience is often an issue. Work experience can be crucial in this respect and this includes volunteering which is often the only way to gain experience in certain fields. You may have to have a job that 'pays the bills' and fit in some volunteering to get experience in the field you want to move into.

The process is the same whether you are 16 or 60 and we know it has worked with clients at both ends of the age spectrum.

ADRIAN ARNOLD CASE STUDY

My father had been a very successful chartered accountant and I decided by the age of 15 to pursue a career in a completely different field to avoid any unfavourable comparison. I had always been fascinated by medicine but I wanted to be a bit different so chose veterinary surgery as a profession.

Having graduated from Cambridge University I entered general practice treating both farm and domestic animals. Within a couple of years I realised that my true love was surgery where the patients got better because of what I did rather than in spite of what I did.

I decided to set up my own practice in Crawley which was an expanding town in need of another veterinary practice. Within a few years it had become a three-person practice specialising in small animal medicine. As the practice grew it became more profitable but, after 12 years, I began to lose the personal relationship I had enjoyed with my clients. The job satisfaction began to dip so, after considerable family discussion, we decided to up sticks and start a new practice in Colchester – a part of the country I had known as a teenager. I retained my partnership in the Crawley practice while the Colchester practice got off the ground.

Computers were just beginning to become available to small businesses at the time and I got my first Apple machine to cope with the financial side of the business so that I could spend more of my time practising veterinary surgery. In 1980 computing software tailored for use in medical and veterinary practices became more widely available. I saw this as a further opportunity to reduce the logistical burden of writing case histories, itemising bills, offering quotations for future work and creating mailing lists for newsletters and vaccination reminders. This all made the practice more efficient and more profitable and gave me time to develop my interest in home computing.

Unfortunately, in the mid-80s, I developed depression which became increasingly difficult to manage. I was also beginning to feel that there had been too much of a swing away from the 'art' of veterinary medicine towards the impersonal 'science'. My job satisfaction began to wane and I decided to take early retirement at the age of 57. Where to go from here?

One of the pleasures of my veterinary life had been the interaction with people on a one-to-one basis. I was not really interested in how computers worked but what they could do. There was a whole generation of parents out there whose children's computing skills were beginning to leave them feeling isolated. I was self-taught in the use of computers and had made all the mistakes of a beginner – and even some that experts had never thought of! Small advertisements in local publications soon had enthusiastic parents knocking on my door and happy to pay a commercial rate for tuition. I began to create notes on various computing subjects that I could print out on the pupil's machine leaving them with a hard copy that they could refer to when trying out their new skills.

I was aware of the many computing handbooks on the market but most were written in 'computer speak' with an unhelpful seasoning of acronyms. There was a market for a textbook written in light, humorous English which did not address the reader as either an IT student or a dimwit.

My book proposal was taken up by John Wiley & Sons and the book was published in October 2008. So far it has sold more than 7,500 copies worldwide with a request to translate it into Lithuanian! Since that time I have written two follow-up books which will be in the bookshops by the time that this book goes go press.

I am now 70 years old and actively following up an idea for a series of children's books based on stories I have invented for my grandchildren. If I were to offer one piece of advice, it would be that problems are only opportunities in disguise – sheep in wolves' clothing.

23. Portfolio careers

'Variety's the very spice of life / That gives it all its flavour'
WILLIAM COWPER, English poet

Over the past 10 years, we have seen a continued growth in the field of portfolio working that often offers those we are working with an opportunity to find the exact match for them. Both of us have portfolio careers and haven't looked back since we started this different type of working – although having said that, our portfolio careers are still very different from each other's.

A portfolio career is one that is made up of a series of jobs or pieces of work that run concurrently rather than focusing on just one career that moves you progressively up the ranks of your chosen profession. A portfolio worker is often self-employed, offering a range of skills, or takes part-time employment with a few different employers.

For many people, having a portfolio career is the way to integrate their various interests into their working life or a practical solution to enable them to follow their dream. Having a portfolio career might mean that for three days of the week you do a job to pay the bills and then the other two days you are able to do work that pays less but gives you greater satisfaction or helps move you towards your long-term goal. It can be a great way to work in several different chosen fields and maintain a sense of independence and variety in your work life.

There are so many reasons why people choose to consider a portfolio career – they may be seeking a greater work/life balance; they may want a greater variety in what they do, to explore different aspects of their skill set; they may want to avoid working for someone else again full-time – the list is endless.

Would a portfolio career suit you?

The idea of a portfolio career can be very compelling but there are various things that you should bear in mind if you are thinking about this as an option:

- It is important that you maintain a strategic direction for your career – look at your portfolio as a unified whole with a direction and progression rather than as a collection of jobs that pay the mortgage.
- What activities are going to make up your portfolio? Are they viable money-making options or will some part of your portfolio be about pursuing an area of interest?
- Do you have the time to devote to each area of your portfolio?
- Work out your household expenditure. It's really important not to underestimate the amount of money you need as this will impact heavily on the portfolio mix you are aiming for – see if this is realistic or not.
- Are you happy working alone? Often, a portfolio career will mean working on your own for long periods of time and many people find that this doesn't suit their personality type at all.
- How will you go about finding work? Many employers are not comfortable about employing part-time workers – can you make a compelling case for going part-time? If you are going to be a freelance consultant or have your own business, do you have the skills to go out and sell yourself? If in doubt, work out how you would sell £100 worth of your product or time – if you struggle knowing how you would raise that amount of money, how are you going to create a solid income stream?
- Are you comfortable with uncertainty? One of the benefits of a full-time role is that you often have the feeling of security in the role (although many of you reading this may have discovered the hard way that there is very little security in full-time work if you have been made redundant). Constantly finding time to market yourself and deliver the work you do can be difficult – finding a balance between the two is vital.
- What additional 'protection' will you need? Most companies provide benefits for employees and if you become a portfolio worker, you

will need to consider whether you will provide these for yourself, for example, critical illness cover, mortgage protection, or private health insurance?

- Are you organised? If this comes naturally to you, you are very lucky. If this is more of a challenge – think about the demands of paying bills, invoicing clients, keeping your insurances up to date, delivering on time to clients etc. – then organisational skills are something you may want to get under control early on.
- Do you have a good support network? As you get started, you may feel nervous and, at times, isolated. Having supportive family and friends around you to help you maintain your momentum can be the difference between success and a return to your old job.
- Are you ready to become a networking expert? Once again, your ability to research and meet like-minded individuals who are also pursuing a portfolio career for advice and guidance will come to the fore. Refer back to the networking section on developing business leads within your community and through the networks you already have.

If you are determined, you will find a way to make a portfolio career work. For some, that might mean taking on one part-time job that pays your living expenses and having one day a week to accept work from referral networks you have set up (e.g. friends and family who might refer people to you).

The hardest part is getting started and established. If you are good at what you do and are professional in how you approach it, you will start to build up a good reputation and gather referrals. If you decide this is the option for you, keep working at it until you can find a balance of activities that work for you. You may make a few turns along the way that don't work but if you have a good balance in your portfolio, you can readjust to find a turn that does.

Jane set up a mail order eco-friendly products business a few years ago but still needed to work in her career coaching business to bring in the money to pay the mortgage. She found the mail order business took over most of her time and standing on a stall at the weekends selling her products through fairs and shows encroached too much on her family time. In the end, after much consideration, she closed the company down as it did not make enough money to justify the huge amount of time she was putting into it.

Over the years, we have come across so many permutations of the portfolio career that have worked well for those who have undertaken them – perhaps a few of their stories will provide some inspiration:

- Jim works four days a week as a dentist in a private practice which enables him to take a day off in the working week and go hiking, biking or climbing in the highlands.
- Jane took a three days a week contract with a trade union to set up a career coaching service for their members, leaving the other two days free to set up her own company and find other clients.
- Gemma and Paul work on short-term contracts (their most recent was working at a Christmas attraction) and then at a ski resort in Canada for the rest of the time.
- Tony works as a management consultant for nine months each year and then takes three months off to pursue a new interest. Those interests have included writing a book, cycling through Europe and learning to ski.
- Chris works as a freelance HR consultant and also has a livery stable that he runs with his partner.
- Jane works as a part-time bookkeeper and is retraining as a physiotherapist.
- Cora is an actor and also runs a business training executives on presentation skills and communication.
- Tim writes books on personal development, advises large corporates on their HR policy (he has a background in strategic HR in financial services) and is on the speaking circuit.

KATE CLIFFORD CASE STUDY

Since school I have always been interested in travelling and non-profit sector work, and for that reason I did volunteer work in South Africa before and after university. At school I was also keen to specialise in something I considered a practical career, so I chose to study engineering. After graduating and two years of volunteer work, even though I was still interested in social issues and working internationally, I was advised and decided that getting some solid professional experience in engineering was worthwhile and would give me flexibility in future.

I really enjoyed working and living in London as a structural engineer in my 20s, and certainly learned a lot that was practical and transferable, but I was never fully satisfied. Completing a part-time Master's degree helped me to get a broader professional qualification in urban development, focusing on developing countries, and I was determined to shift my career in that direction.

My first choice was to shift incrementally, so while remaining UK-based I aimed for urban development consultancy work, but gradually built up my CV and looked for international opportunities. I started on this path and my first opening was with my existing employer looking at business opportunities for the company in developing countries plus getting some experience with colleagues in urban design and planning, and also in partnering with local authorities. However, within just a few months I realised I wasn't progressing or getting into the substance of the work that would really interest me.

At this point I really wanted to branch out more professionally and test myself in different kinds of roles and environments, but didn't see an obvious path or employer. With Camilla's help, I took note of another long-term goal – to work for myself, for the freedom it could offer, so the big step for me was taking the plunge to go freelance.

I had a plan, but not a very detailed or extensive one; I think the key was to open myself up to opportunities. The most important advice I received was to have a plan, to give myself some structure, but to take any opportunity on its merits and be ready to throw the plan out the window! I did, and, having barely written even an essay in my very maths/engineering/design focused education, found myself utterly unexpectedly writing a guide for local government and managing case-study research on cities around the world. It was hugely refreshing, and recognising and embracing it as a massive change meant that I resisted measuring too much if it was the 'right' step on a career ladder or whether I had the necessary credentials.

It also opened up a world of new contacts that resulted in me undertaking several contracts in humanitarian work with the UN in Afghanistan, Sudan and Indonesia – some incredible experiences. The lesson I feel has served me best since going freelance was realising that what counted as much or more than my technical expertise was my character and relationships, my attitude to approaching new tasks and roles, and believing that there was little to lose in trying! That lesson spreads far beyond my career change; I met my partner in Afghanistan, and we currently live in Costa Rica, managing our own businesses. Based on my experiences I am also starting to coach those working in international development and the non-profit sector. The career change experience and understanding how and why I made my decisions were the foundation for the diverse life I have created for myself now that suits me really well.

24. Starting your own business

'It always seems impossible until it's done.'
NELSON MANDELA, former President of South Africa

Perhaps having a portfolio career feels too indiscriminate and lacking a clear direction but you are drawn by some of the ideas discussed above. Perhaps, then, may be having your own business with a clear focus to make an income would work better for you.

It is crucial that you do your research when setting up a business and work out your master plan. It's important to define what success means to you and where you are heading. The things that can be so important in determining our happiness in a career can also affect you when setting up a business.

Setting up your own enterprise can be a lonely and risky endeavour. The rewards can be great but you need to understand whether it will suit you.

Reviewing your career can also mean that you are clear about what your priorities are – and these can change, affecting when, and if, you seek funding.

Jane's highest priority is having control of her time and this has meant that she has actively never sought funding, because she always felt it would have put her under too much pressure from investors to deliver financial results. The downside of this is that the business hasn't been able to grow as much as perhaps it could have.

Completing Part Two and undertaking the research that comes from that may encourage you to consider whether it is time to set up a business either now or in the future. Perhaps you've had enough of working for someone else or you have a compelling business idea that you think has legs and which you want to pursue. As part of your consideration of what's next, if owning your own business is a possibility then it is well worth exploring whether, as with any possible new avenue, it will work for you.

Exploring options

By completing the process outlined in Part Two you will understand what is important to you and what you have to offer. This will help you in working out what team to surround yourself with as you will be able to see the gaps in your skill set.

Additional research will help you understand the pros and cons, to see what you need to do to decide whether starting your own business is the right move for you. Several clients we have worked with have decided that it is right in the long term for them to set up a business and this has affected the decisions they have taken in the short term.

Having said that, setting up a business doesn't have to be an 'all or nothing approach' and it is worth considering the following:

- **Could you approach your current employer about setting up a new area of business? This might give you the security of a regular pay cheque while taking you in a new direction. They may even end up being your biggest client initially.**
- **Can you gain training or experience in a new area in your current**

work by putting yourself forward for new projects or pitching new opportunities for the business?

- You might be able to set up your business part-time or take a contract initially to see if your idea has legs and enable you to keep money coming in to pay the bills.
- Your partner may be able to support you while you set up the business – a 'piggy back' approach.

Sometimes the only option is to jump in with both feet and start a business. We have found that this always seems to take longer than you think especially if you are used to a regular pay cheque; it can be an unwelcome surprise to learn that not everyone pays on time! So make sure you have some financial reserves to get you through the early stages of setting up a business, and a good relationship with the bank for those inevitable lean periods.

SARAH CURRAN CASE STUDY

I moved down to London after finishing a business and finance course at college at the age of 18. I knew that I wanted to go straight into work rather than take the university route. At such a young age I really did not know what career I wanted. In fact it was only at 30 that I discovered my passion was to lead me into fashion retail. My career throughout my 20s was working in PA or administrative roles. The one thing I always made sure of was that I loved the companies I worked for – I've always felt that we spend so much time working, that it's important to love what you do. The moment I dreaded going into work was usually when I knew it was time to move on. In 10 years I only had three main jobs. I was extremely loyal and dedicated to the companies I worked for which ranged from French steel importers to L'Oreal and finally News International, where I stayed for nearly five years. Work was very much linked to my personal life and I always developed strong relationships with colleagues.

I met Andrew, my husband, at 28. He was an entrepreneur with a growing business in London. I left News International just before getting married in July 2002 but after six months of not working, I felt I needed to set myself a challenge. In 2003 I decided to open a fashion boutique close to where we were living in North London. Fashion had always been more than just clothing; I recall trying to make a 'Jackie O' style jacket at the age of 15 with no pattern to follow – needless to say it was a mess. With Andrew's help I got a £100k bank loan, and opened Powder. My major transition occurred as I hit 30, following the birth of my first child Jake. I realised that in order to have the lifestyle I wanted for the family, rather than leave it to Andrew to provide alone, I needed to contribute. What started as one local fashion boutique, turned into a desire to build a global fashion e-tail brand, with aggressive sales targets and an ambitious exit plan. Andrew and I launched my-wardrobe.com together in April 2006.

For the first 18 months the team grew from two to 30. This started to bring with it the usual staffing issues of managing people; I had never had experience in managing a team, and there was an expectation for me to move into the CEO role following the first round of funding. My main issue was that as the business was growing and more experienced directors joined, my confidence in my own ability to lead the business seemed to diminish. One thing I was totally confident about was my vision for the brand and the direction I wanted us to take. It was at this point that I started my coaching sessions.

I must admit to being extremely nervous during the first session. I worried that my coach would see through me but very quickly relaxed. I recall Camilla telling me that one day I would wake up and feel confident enough to continue without the regular sessions with her. I remember thinking at that point that it would never happen but Camilla's advice was 'fake it 'til you make it'. I did that until one day I realised that I was no longer faking it, and I had developed the confidence to lead the business. Furthermore, I no longer felt I needed the regular sessions. I'm sure that as we enter the next stage of the business's growth I will need Camilla's help again. I believe this to be an evolving career development.

My advice to anyone would be to follow what you love doing. It has taken a lot of sacrifice, financially and personally, but I am passionate about the business; I love what we do and am proud of what we have developed. We now have a team of 70 people in two locations and an expected turnover of £9m this year. Working with Andrew has made it easier, as we often support one another when the other has one of those days when we question 'what are we doing?'. If you love what you do, and you're passionate, a lot of the time it won't feel like work. I am lucky that I feel privileged to do what I do. I also feel proud of the massive career transformation which has occurred over the past six years. The coaching was a major part of that transformation.

Top tips

Jane set up her business over 10 years ago and has worked with numerous clients who have decided to follow a similar route. Listed below are some of their key learning points:

- Outsource what you're not good at as soon as possible, leaving you to focus on what value you bring to the company.
- In a similar vein, recognise what skills you need to recruit – a common trap is to recruit people like you with similar skills.
- Decide on the long-term strategy of the business – easier said than done especially if you have partners with different objectives or these objectives change due to personal circumstances. Review this regularly.
- Setting up a business can involve personal sacrifice as well as rewards, and only you know whether it is worth it. Review the values exercise in Part Two on a regular basis.
- Often you can be so busy delivering at the coalface that you don't have time to look up and think about where the business is going – put time in your diary to do this.
- Consider whether your business is scalable and if this is what you want. Do you want to have an exit strategy?
- What funding do you need? Who are you going to approach? What's in it for them?
- Consider your own personality and whether it is suited to the world of self-employment/business ownership – are you persistent enough, are you happy to work on your own initially, are you self-motivated?

Free advice is often available from banks and more impartial advice from governmental enterprise organisations as most governments are keen to encourage entrepreneurialism, especially when it creates jobs.

There is a whole raft of books written about setting up a business and we suggest that you do as much research as you can before you decide whether this is for you. Something else that can be helpful is to consider who your role models are and then read the biographies of the people who have been there and done that very thing.

Want to be an inventor? Read the biographies of famous inventors like James Dyson; want to set up a zoo? Read about Gerald Durrell who set up Jersey Zoo. You get the picture! Unless you are thinking about doing something really different then most of the time there are books out there that will give you insight into the type of business you want to set up. Hopefully these people will inspire you.

If you are considering the possibility of being self-employed or a business owner, it is important to point out that it is not the easy option. At the end of the day there are no guarantees that your business idea will work out **but** if you do some focused thinking and research then you will be ahead of the majority of people who set up businesses, putting you in a better position to succeed.

25. How to choose a career coach

Career coaching

Despite the very best of intentions as you work your way through this book, you may find the going tough, lose momentum or find that your support team has fallen by the wayside. We know that while it is possible to work your way through the book to get to the answers you are looking for, sometimes it can be useful to have an experienced helping hand to give you guidance, advice and renew your enthusiasm. At that point, you may consider going to a career coach. There will be thousands of coaches in your geographic area and many will say that they do career coaching. This section will hopefully go some way to helping you sort the wheat from the chaff, decide what sort of person you want to work with and get the coaching relationship working well for you.

Coaching is definitely an investment. A good coach is all about you and your specific needs and while they may have a process that they follow, if you and a friend were being coached by someone good, you would have very different experiences as coaching addresses what you need rather than a generic set of rules that are followed regardless. For coaching to be at its most effective, two components are vital: the ability of the coach and the 100 per cent commitment of the person being coached. If you are not fully committed, take some time to work out why and what you can do to get past it. Don't start coaching until you are absolutely ready.

How to choose the right career coach for you

Once you have decided to explore career coaching as an option, it is worth asking around your network if anyone has worked successfully with a coach or knows someone who has. If not, you can contact one of the coaching organisations or contact us at **www.howtotakechargeofyourcareer.com** to work with us or to get the name or names of some suitable coaches who specialise in careers coaching rather than generalist coaches.

Before you start, it is worth asking yourself a few questions to help you narrow down the sort of person you are looking for:

- Why are you interested in career coaching right now? E.g. are you lacking motivation, are you struggling to work out the next step, are some of your limiting beliefs getting in the way?
- What is important to you in finding a career coach? E.g. experience, qualifications, recommendation, personality fit?
- What would convince you to work with someone?
- What would convince you not to work with someone?
- What sort of personality do you work well with? E.g. challenging, supportive, soft, punchy, direct, caring, safe or a combination?
- How might you sabotage the coaching relationship and are you willing to give the coach permission to call you on it? E.g. not completing your homework on time, prevaricating etc.
- How much are you willing to invest in the coaching process financially (i.e. how much can you pay per session)?
- Are you doing this for you or is someone bribing, cajoling, strongly encouraging you to do it and you feel some reticence? If the latter, you are unlikely to get what you want out of the coaching process.

We would always advise that you talk to at least two coaches, even if someone has come highly recommended, so that you can get a feel for the different approaches that coaches use and who would be best to work with you. We can't think of any coach who would not agree to this free initial conversation to discuss why you are looking for coaching, to find out a little about you and to go into some detail about how they work.

If you go to a coaching company, make sure that when it comes to having an introductory conversation, you are having it with the person who will be your coach, not a sales person for the company. If they are reluctant to let you do that, move on!

Once you have a couple of names to contact, arrange an introductory conversation. It is useful if you can tell them up front what you would like to focus on and a little bit about yourself – areas might include:

- An overview of your story so the coach can get a sense of you and how you describe yourself and your background.
- Areas you would particularly like to focus on with coaching – where are you getting stuck? What behaviours or beliefs are getting in your way?
- How you would know that the coaching has been successful?
- How much do you know about coaching – have you been coached before and if so, what worked well for you and what didn't work so well?

During the conversation there are quite a few things to think about that might help you make up your mind about who you want to work with:

- Having decided what is important to you about the coach you are going to work with, make sure you cover all those areas during the meeting.
- Coaches will have different styles/approaches to coaching so these introductory meetings are a chance for you to see which will work best for you.
- Ask as many questions as you can – this is your opportunity to find out how the coaches work and whether you think their approach will work for you.

- We strongly suggest that you choose the coach who you feel is the best equipped to address your reason(s) for coaching. This may not necessarily be the person you liked the most or felt most comfortable with, although that shouldn't be entirely dismissed!
- If the coaches you meet don't seem to fit with what you're looking for, it is worth checking that what you think you want really reflects what you are trying to achieve. You might also want to think about whether you are really ready to make a commitment to coaching at the moment. If you feel sure about all of that, it's time to talk to another coach.
- Talk about any concerns you have about coaching with each coach you meet to see how they address them. The more honest you are from the very start, the more effective the coaching will be.

The people we recommend have a career coaching specialism and have extensive experience working in this field. Sadly we have found that accreditation and qualifications don't always guarantee excellent coaching and many coaches will agree to take on a client regardless of their level of experience in a particular specialism.

It depends what you particularly want to focus on with your coach but if it is the whole career change process, it makes sense to work with someone who has done this many times and is very confident in the field. If it is a particular limiting belief that is getting in your way, a coach with a broader skill set will be able to help. If in doubt, ask them to talk you through some examples of similar coaching assignments they have undertaken recently.

Finally – trust your gut! If it feels right, if they have the experience and you are ready to commit – go for it. If you start working with the coach and it isn't right for you, for whatever reason – if you feel it is fixable, tell the coach (back to the honesty!) but if you feel it is a deeper problem, end the coaching relationship.

Cost and number of sessions

Coaching session costs vary hugely depending on many different factors including geography, experience of the coach, whether you are paying as an individual or your company is paying, and so on. Do your research at the outset to work out what the going rate is for both face-to-face coaching (more expensive) and telephone coaching (cheaper and more time flexible) and work out what you can afford to pay. If you are going to do this, look at it as an investment; you may find the coaching gives you insights into how you can use the same methods to advance in other areas of your life and will give you a way forward for planning your career.

Coaches charge in a whole range of different ways. If you are quoted a price for a fixed programme, find out what that will cover. It is also worth asking how much any additional sessions would be if you wanted to continue the coaching and whether you can continue with the same coach. With coaches who charge per session, it might be worth asking if they offer a discount if you buy a series of sessions together (for example, paying for the first three sessions up front). If you go to a company that specialises in career coaching, compare their prices with those of individual coaches to make sure you are getting a good price. Some of the larger specialist coaching companies have large staffs, premises etc. which can boost the price per session so it is worth checking!

We would advise that you agree to at least three sessions – in that time frame you should definitely be feeling progress and have confidence that you know where you are heading. If not, tell the coach. From that point on, only you and the coach can decide how long the process will take. Some people like to do the coaching in stages (first stage to decide on a new career direction and start research; second stage putting the research and networking into action; third stage making the move, and so on) and others like to continue the momentum. Some people we have worked with have come up with their career change action plan within three sessions, others have taken six or 12 depending on the limiting beliefs or difficulties that can get in the way. It is not a race – it is about getting to the right place in the right time frame for you.

How to get the most out of coaching

Over the years, we have seen that the people who get the most from coaching do all or most of the following things:

- They understand that the coach is a facilitator and will not be giving them the answers but will be asking questions, giving feedback and eliciting different thoughts or thinking patterns to help create change. Sadly they don't have a magic wand with the answer to your career conundrum!
- They are keen to get the most from their coaching and if they do have any concerns or things that just don't feel right, they articulate them early on in the coaching relationship.
- They show up at each session, ready to focus, having done all the things they agreed to do at the last meeting and having thought through what specifically they would like to cover in that session.
- They give regular feedback to the coach on how they feel the coaching is progressing and how they feel it could be more effective. (If you are uncomfortable with the idea of giving feedback, discuss this with the coach as soon as possible so you can deal with this early on).
- If they decide that the coaching is not working for them (because the coach is not right, coaching is not the right intervention or they cannot give the time required to the process), they say so and call a halt to the coaching.
- They complete all the work to be undertaken between sessions in a measured way (as opposed to the day before!) and are ready to give feedback to their coach on what has worked well and what has been less effective – i.e. they practise and research!
- They are open to having their thinking challenged by the coach and keep an open mind.
- They will contact the coach between sessions to discuss an issue that has arisen or anything that is impeding progress so that the momentum is maintained.
- They have fun with the coaching – it can be challenging, have its difficult moments and requires dedication but it should also be fun.

PART FOUR: JOB SEARCH STRATEGY – GETTING INTERVIEWS AND SECURING THE JOB

'To succeed in life in today's world, you must have the will and tenacity to finish the job.'

CHIN-NING CHU, author and speaker

We are now on the home stretch. Our hope is that if you have followed the exercises throughout the book you have:

- become aware of any self-limiting beliefs or people you have around you and have found a way to keep them under control as you consider what's next in terms of your career;
- an overview of your verifiable skill sets for the workplace and have a clear understanding of what you are looking for in your ideal work situation;
- brainstormed various options that are worthy of exploration to check out a range of different sectors, careers, working styles;
- undertaken both active and passive research to verify whether these brainstormed options are viable for you in your current circumstances and have narrowed down your future career action plan to one or possible two specific targets;
- an action plan of how you are going to move forward with these options.

So now comes the obvious next stage: the job search strategy. During Part Four, we will outline for you the tried and tested techniques on the basics of a job search. As with all things, you can complicate and write huge tracts on each aspect of the job search – indeed, you may well have come across huge tomes on each subject area. What we have endeavoured to do is to break down each aspect into manageable and easily achievable chunks that we have seen work time and again.

26. What you want from a career versus what an employer wants from you

'You know you are on the road to success if you would do your job, and not be paid for it.'

OPRAH WINFREY, American talk show host, actress, producer and philanthropist

It may sound obvious but one of the things that so many candidates fail to appreciate is that what they are looking for in a new role is often not necessarily what an employer is looking for to fill the role. You may well have identified that you want additional responsibility, an opportunity to advance, increased salary and benefits, work/life balance perhaps, and so your list will continue – look at your matrix for your personal list. From an employer's point of view they may well have a distinctly different list of requirements when they are filling a role which might include someone to solve their immediate problems in the business, a square peg to fit a square hole, someone to save and/or make them money, a fully committed worker and ultimately someone who will make the employer's job easier.

There is room to satisfy both sets of needs but it is important to bear in mind as you start your job search that when you meet a potential employer, you should focus on their needs rather than yours and what you can bring to the job not what you are personally going to get out of it. We will focus more on this during our overview of giving a good interview but it is a good rule of thumb to keep it in the back of your mind in all your interactions – What can I do for you? rather than, What are you going to provide for me?

27. Applying for jobs

The job market is huge. Even in a downturn there are new opportunities constantly appearing, you just need to know where to look. Most job seekers rush around like headless chickens applying for everything and anything. A more effective approach is when clients target what they are looking for using routes to market which fewer people use.

In the following chapters we have outlined a range of different strategies for your job search and encourage you to look at a variety of approaches to achieve your goal of a new role. There are two key aspects to the job market – the traditional open market (applying for jobs through advertisements and recruiters) and the hidden market (finding jobs through networking and speculative applications). According to a study by Drake Beam Morin, a world leading provider of strategic human resource solutions, 64 per cent of the people surveyed said they found their new jobs through networking. This figure is commonly cited by recruiters and outplacement firms which is why we have started with that as our first recommended strategy.

Companies want to keep their recruitment costs down (which can be up to 33 per cent of an employee's annual salary in some cases) and they want to hire 'known' quantities – people who have been recommended to them, who they have seen in action or who have an excellent reputation in the market. As well as a potential reduction in cost, a direct approach from a motivated candidate who has done their research or a recommended candidate reduces the risk for the employer of hiring the wrong person, resulting in a quicker hire with less time spent filtering out unsuitable candidates.

28. Networking

'It's not what you know but who you know that makes the difference.'

Anonymous

First, it is important that your networking is targeted as networking without any kind of focus will generally be a waste of your time.

By this stage in your research, you will have a list of organisations you want to target in your chosen sector. For each company, find out if there is someone there you know or, if not, look at your research for possible contacts you have come across.

While we are advocates of using business networking sites and have seen clients gain projects, consulting work and jobs through these sites, it can be all too easy to hide behind them. There really is no substitute for meeting people face-to-face, as this really can progress your career.

When you arrange a networking meeting, it is useful to approach it as a business meeting where both you and the person you have arranged to meet will benefit. They might have important information about the industry, firm or even potential job opportunities that could be vital to your job search but they may also benefit themselves. The more of these meetings you have, the more information you will gather and, if it is not confidential, you can share that in future meetings to create more of a two-way meeting experience. This is about gathering information, asking for advice and not about asking for a job outright or begging for help!

Marketing and positioning yourself if you have a lead into the company

Once you have found the appropriate contact within your network, ask them for the background information you need on the target organisation (but not information in the public domain), and the name of the person to whom you should address your application. If you are able to refer to your contact in the application letter, so much the better – it will add credibility to your approach. Business networking sites like LinkedIn (**www.linkedin.com**) are useful to help you ascertain whether there is anyone in your network who may be able to help you connect with a contact in your target organisation. However, on a cautionary note, only connect to those you know well or would be happy to help as it becomes awkward when you are asked to introduce someone to a trusted contact you don't know well – the benefits of this useful site then become lost. We list other sites that may be helpful on our website (**www.howtotakechargeofyourcareer.com**)

When approaching people for a networking meeting, it's not advisable to send them a copy of your CV unless they have specifically requested it. A CV can immediately flag up to a networking contact that you are looking for a job; if he or she doesn't have any immediate jobs, they might not see you. At this stage you want to meet them to find out how your skills could meet their needs and so a better approach is to write a carefully crafted introductory letter which emphasises your relevant experience.

We recommend a letter rather than an email (unless the recipient knows you will be emailing them). This is because people are wary of receiving emails from unknown sources and also, given the large volume of emails received by senior and middle managers, your communication may not receive the attention it deserves.

As a guide, if you have relevant past work experience, we advise that your letter follows the following format:

- The first paragraph introduces you and states the name of the person in your network who has provided the introduction.
- The second paragraph comments on an area of interest, which you have identified in your research that the company is currently facing (perhaps you've noticed they have just launched a new service or expanded their operations in a new location).
- The third paragraph states how your past work experience is relevant in connection with the area of interest.
- The final paragraph details how you are going to follow up for the purpose of organising a meeting or conversation.

If you don't have relevant past experience, you can use the above format but in the third paragraph you should refer to either the project/internship/volunteer work you have done or you are planning to do and how it is relevant to them.

Follow-up tips

You should follow up after sending a letter ideally about a week after it has been sent. Any earlier and you might look pushy, any later and they might have forgotten about you.

Following up with a phone call will increase your chances of getting a meeting. A simple technique for overcoming voicemail is to leave just one message stating that you are following up from your letter. If they don't return your message after a few days, keep calling them until you get hold of them, but don't leave a message if you get voicemail again. If you keep leaving messages you might be perceived as a nuisance. A secretary or PA can help you get in touch with them if you are polite and ask for the best time to ring in order to get hold of the person.

Another strategy is to call early in the morning or late in the evening. You may have more luck getting through to the person you want to speak to, and if you have encountered an unhelpful secretary or PA, he or she is less likely to be there.

If you are successful in securing a meeting, how do you get the most out of this precious opportunity?

Meeting tips

- Always arrive on time and be aware of what you want to get out of the meeting.
- At the outset reiterate who you are, why you are there and who has suggested you get in touch to create a shared point of contact. It is useful to have an outlined agenda of the meeting in your head before you start so that you know what you want to cover and preferably in what order. This will allow you to cover all the important areas during your meeting whilst also finishing on time.
- Your mission for the meeting is to find out if there are any potential jobs or recommended ways into the business and if so, how to pursue those opportunities.
- Be sure to ask as much as possible about them and the issues facing the company so you can work out how to position yourself. Do your research before the meeting to prepare some good and pertinent questions.
- Like an informational interview, if you've said that you will only take up 20-30 minutes of their time, it is up to you to keep track of the meeting and make sure you stick to the time frame you have requested.
- At the end of your meeting, it is always worth asking if there is anyone they could introduce you to, who may be interested in talking to someone with your background. If they do come up with new contacts, take the initiative and ask them to let their contact know you will be in touch rather than waiting for their contact to get in touch with you. If you say you are going to follow up these leads – make sure you do.

After struggling to make contact with the CEO on the phone John rang at 7.30 one morning and got through. He was invited in for a chat the next day and he assured the CEO he would not take more than 30 minutes of his time. During the meeting John asked lots of questions, one being 'What problems keep you awake at night?' When describing the issues the CEO gave John lots of ideas for projects. He wrote to the CEO after the meeting and put forward a proposal to investigate and present a solution to one of the major problems the company had. This was accepted and at the end of the project John was offered a permanent job.

Always follow up after the meeting with a letter or email to thank the person for their time. Depending on the content of the meeting you might want to mention the issues you covered, write a short proposal on how you could work for them or, if appropriate, reiterate how your experience could assist them. Make sure you keep in touch and send them any information that might help them with their job or a current issue they are facing.

Speculative applications: marketing and positioning yourself if you don't have a lead into the company

The advice regarding the type of letter you should write, the format, how to follow up and how to conduct a meeting is the same as in the section above, except you won't be able to refer to a mutual acquaintance. This means it is even more important to follow up your letters (it will also give you the opportunity to find out if you have sent your letter to the right person). Make sure you personalise a direct approach letter; make reference to changes in the industry, issues the company may be facing or even the fact they have got a new job! Think like a consultant – how can you demonstrate that your skills can help them?

If you are not able to identify a contact within your network who can help you connect with your target company, you will need to make a speculative approach, which is a direct approach to someone you don't know. Contacting people 'cold' is a method that many of our clients have used successfully but you must be realistic and make sure you keep your volume of applications high – this is very much like a sales cycle; you have to feed the pipeline to uncover opportunities. Also, depending on the role you are targeting, e.g a senior position of which there will be fewer, you may need to increase the number of companies you are approaching.

Make sure you are targeting people at the right level for the type of work you wish to do. Ideally aim two levels above the level you want to work at. If in doubt target high but not too high, as a letter that has been passed down from someone senior is more likely to be taken seriously, but a letter written speculatively to the CEO of a large plc is likely to be passed to the human resources department by his or her PA. Bear in mind that you don't want your CV falling into the hands of a manager at your level of seniority who sees that your experience is better than his or hers – it could end up in the bin!

Unless you want to work in human resources, we'd advise you to write to line managers where possible. If the company has a clear recruitment policy then you will need to abide by these rules but otherwise line managers are close to the business and are in a good position to see when job opportunities might arise in their departments. A senior marketing manager within a well known plc told us that she keeps all good unsolicited CVs and meets some people for a coffee as she never knows when she might need good people in her team.

Make sure you are regularly scanning the press (including industry magazines) for articles connected with the companies in your target list. This can give you an appropriate contact name, as senior people are often quoted in articles.

Other places to find the names of senior executives include:

- The press and magazines related to the industry in which you are interested. It is also worth noting that people new in position may be open to recruiting new people.
- The company's annual report.
- The company's website.
- Speaker lists from industry conferences.

- LinkedIn (www.linkedin.com). Search on company and job titles and scan testimonials given by managers of people working for the target company as they will often lead you to more names.

29. Advertising

'Advertising says to people, Here's what we've got. Here's what it will do for you. Here's how to get it.'
LEO BURNETT, advertising pioneer

Responding to job advertisements is the most obvious way of getting a job, but it is also the most competitive. With the advent of Internet advertising, employers get hundreds if not thousands of applications.

If you are looking for a role that builds directly on your current experience then responding to job advertisements should be an important part of your strategy. It is also important to consider if you are changing industry, as sometimes transferable functional experience is more important to recruiters than industry experience. However, if you are completely changing career then, unless you're willing to start at the bottom, this method of job hunting should be your lowest priority.

Jobs advertised in newspapers

Although the main newspapers do have websites, it's best to buy the newspaper on the day its appointments section is published as there can be a delay in putting roles on the website.

Newspaper websites have alerting facilities that allow you to register what kind of jobs you are interested in. Matches will be emailed to you as they are placed on the site.

How and why to read job adverts

There are two reasons to read job adverts. The first is obvious: to find that dream role that matches your skills and chosen career perfectly; the second is perhaps less obvious: it can be a great way to keep in touch with the market and can form an important part of your ongoing research.

When you are reading a potential advert that seems to match what you are looking for in your next role, it is worth using a highlighter pen to make sure, when you respond, that you have covered all the key areas. They include:

1. Any reference number or name of the advertisement – make sure you include this in your application so the recruiter knows which job you are applying for.
2. Skills and experience that are essential to the role – highlight each of them so you can make sure that both your cover letter and CV feature those skills prominently.
3. Additional skills and experience that are desired but not essential – if you match them, it is worth highlighting the fact in your application.
4. The application deadline – the sooner you apply the better, but don't miss the deadline.

If you are reading the adverts but not finding the role for you, look at the companies that are advertising in your chosen sector or function. Are they on your list of potential future employers? Do they always recruit directly or through a recruiter? Are you starting to see a recruiter that specialises in your industry who you have not been in touch with? What are the typical salaries being advertised in your chosen field? You never know when an advert might help you spot a new opportunity for your job search.

Application deadlines

The generally accepted timescale for applications is two weeks. Whether the deadline is stated or not, aim to make your application as early as possible. The person recruiting may be under pressure to recruit and may start the process of interviewing as soon as they receive applications meeting their recruiting criteria. If you delay applying, even if you fully meet the criteria, you may miss out on an interview if the recruiter has already made his or her selection.

30. The world of recruitment companies

Recruitment firms are most interested in people who have relevant experience for the position they are trying to fill. Therefore, these firms will be a useful tool for you if you're looking for a role that builds on your previous experience.

Remember that functional experience (such as finance skills, HR skills etc.) is often transferable across industries, so don't discount recruitment firms if you're looking to stay in the same function but in a new sector.

If you **don't** have a lot of relevant experience, it is likely to be more profitable for you to use networking and speculative applications as your principal methods of job hunting.

It is useful to explain how the recruitment industry works so that you can decide your strategy when dealing with them. When a company decides to recruit via a recruitment firm then the firm will use one or more of the following methods:

Database search	The recruitment firm searches their database of candidate CVs to find a match for the open position (typically used for lower level positions).
Advertised selection	The recruitment firm places an advertisement in a relevant publication or on the Web (used at all levels for positions with salaries of up to about £100,000).
Search/Headhunting	The recruitment firm directly approaches (headhunts) individuals (typically used for senior positions, where the appointment is sensitive, or for skills that are difficult to find). The individuals approached are usually well

known within their industry, or are identified by researchers working for the recruitment firm.

Companies who specialise in recruitment are generally split into two different 'camps' – agencies who do something called contingent recruitment, i.e. they are paid only if one of the candidates they have introduced is hired, and search firms who are paid an ongoing retainer for the research phase as well as the introduction of the successful candidate.

All recruiters, but in particular executive search consultants, receive many unsolicited letters and CVs, and relatively few people who approach them are invited in for interview. This is why, if you have an introduction to a search consultant we suggest you use it, as you are then more likely to be invited in for a chat.

Who the recruitment firm represents

A common misconception is that the recruitment firm is there to represent your best interests as a candidate. Over the years, we have heard many people express bemusement at the lack of attention they get from their recruiter unless they look like they are a 'sure thing' to get the job they have been put forward for. It is important to remember, however, that you are not the client. You are just one of many candidates they have access to and can introduce. As it's the company recruiting that pays the bill, they are considered by the recruitment firm to be the client and that is where they focus their attention. You are, with the best will in the world, a commodity. It is your job to show them how valuable a commodity you are, to maintain contact and help them in their job to retain and impress their paying client.

The fee paid to a recruiter is usually a percentage of the successful candidate's annual starting salary – typically 20 per cent for database (the percentage often increases with salary), 25 per cent for Advertised Selection and 33 per cent for Search/Headhunt. Another reason why a direct approach can often be a cost-effective option for hiring great candidates!

It may be a contentious thing to say and clearly this is not true of all recruitment consultants but because they are rewarded by the number of people that they place in employment, this is where their focus is almost always centered. Many candidates have hopes that a recruiter will also offer careers guidance and, occasionally, think outside the box in terms of the roles they are put forward for. This rarely happens and often leads candidates to feel that they have not had a great service from their recruiters. Again, remember that you are not the client – you are a very useful piece of the puzzle if you have the skills they are looking for. If you understand the key drivers of most recruiters, it is easier to limit **your** expectations and help them provide the right candidate to their client – you!

The best headhunters to approach

Most recruitment firms are organised into specialist functions – e.g. IT, marketing, finance – and then each consultant within the firm will specialise in certain industry sectors.

The International Directory of Executive Recruitment published by Executive Grapevine (**www.askgrapevine.com**) lists the main firms and individuals in the recruitment industry and can help you find recruitment firms who specialise in the function, industry and location you are targeting.

This is available in the reference section of most major libraries but remember that directories go out of date quickly, so the best way to work out who you should register with is to use your own research. Ask people in the industry or function that you want to work in who they use and who they rate in the market place – again, it helps if you have a 'warm' lead to the recruiter by mentioning that one of their clients has suggested you call.

Even if you are not looking to be hired at the moment, keep a file of advertisements for the type of roles you are interested in. Make a note of the name of the recruitment consultant if it is given, as often when a consultant moves on he/she will keep the client relationship. In the recruitment industry, consultants may move companies frequently – often moving on to recruit at a higher level

– so you need to keep track of where the people who recruit in your field are working.

Recruitment consultants also often work on assignments which are never advertised, so it is worth trying to develop a relationship with the key players so that they think of you when a suitable role comes up, either as a candidate or as a potential source of information about where they can find the ideal candidate. Building these relationships will be useful for your whole career. There are thousands of recruitment firms so you must be selective, contacting only those that are relevant to you.

If you are trying to change function as well as industry, remember that you should use both networking and the writing of speculative applications to get a job as recruiters are unlikely to be able or willing to help.

Tips for dealing with recruitment firms

Most reputable recruitment firms follow best practice; however, it is wise to ask them to contact you before they send out your CV. This is to make sure they don't send your CV to a company that you are already trying to contact through networking or direct marketing. This can sometimes happen and may result in your new employer having to haggle about whether they have to pay a fee to the recruitment firm who may claim to have introduced you.

If you are looking to use your relevant experience, recruitment consultants are constantly active in the market, and know which companies are hiring. As with any industry, there are bad consultants, but, contrary to popular belief, there are great ones too and they are certainly an important potential route to getting the job you want.

Marketing and positioning yourself with recruitment firms

When you have selected the recruitment firms which are most appropriate to you, send them a copy of your CV which is specifically targeted to the job you want to secure. In your covering letter you should state what role you are seeking and where you wish to work. Giving this information saves time and helps the recruiter consider you in relation to what his or her clients might be looking for.

Make sure you include what salary you were on in your last role as you will be asked about this, and make sure you clearly state any geographical restrictions you have, which saves time all around.

Again, your covering letter must clearly state what you could do for the recruiter's clients making it easy for the recruiter to 'sell' you in.

31. Covering letters

'Grammar is the grave of letters.'
ELBERT HUBBARD, American writer, artist and philosopher

A covering letter (i.e. a letter or email you send in response to an advertisement or potential job situation to accompany your CV) is an important aspect of your application. It is your chance to establish why you are writing and encourages the interviewer to turn the page and read your CV. It is your chance to highlight the skills you have that match the skills the interviewer is looking for and why you would be an ideal candidate to meet.

The letter will be similar to those you might write for networking or to secure a meeting via a direct contact, however, in this case you know what the interviewer is looking for. Interviewers have a very short period of time to make a decision about whether to invite you in for a meeting so it is imperative that you are very clear about how you meet the recruitment criteria.

We recommend that covering letters should be one page in length, to the point, and should ideally follow the format below.

- The first paragraph explains what job you have applied for and why you have applied.
- The second briefly summarises your background.
- The third paragraph highlights the skills you have that match what the company is looking for.

- **The fourth paragraph gives any extra information asked for in the advertisement.**
- **The final paragraph is your sign off and says that you will either contact them or request they contact you to arrange an interview or to discuss next steps.**

The third paragraph is the most important; a useful way of presenting this information in an easy-to-read format is by using bullet points. If you meet every single criterion stated in the advertisement then you can use the 'mirror technique'. Do this by listing the required attributes on the left-hand side of the page, and then opposite each one show a specific example of how you meet the requirement. When making the list on the left-hand side, try to use the same words and phrases that are used in the advertisement. The mirror technique is beautiful in its simplicity!

For example:

I list below how I meet the criteria for the role:

Strong track record in sales	For the last two years over-achieved sales target by 150 per cent.
International experience	Remotely managed 12 sales staff in Hong Kong, while based in London. Travelled extensively in role as General Manager responsible for EMEA.

If you don't meet all the criteria listed in the advertisement, just list in one column the ones you do meet. Be as specific as possible and avoid vague phrases: recruiters look for hard evidence. This approach can be used for all advertisements and positions that are advertised by recruitment firms.

Most people think of some well worn phrases as to why they want to work for a company – phrases they have lifted off the website – not that impressive! If you want to stand out as a serious candidate demonstrate your in-depth research into the company perhaps by demonstrating your knowledge of their position in the market or a recent piece of positive news about them. Even better is mentioning someone you have taken the time to meet to understand the culture of the company – this really shows you have done your due diligence.

Make sure that you have highlighted key aspects of your experience and skills that are relevant to the role you are applying for. Avoid mentioning any aspects of the job advert that you do not match and refrain from detailing skills that are not relevant to the role or the salary you are looking for unless specifically requested. Always, always check spelling and grammar.

Finally make sure your covering letter isn't too subservient. You should be equal partners in a decision to be hired and your covering letter is a good indication of how high your self-esteem is and whether you have a professional approach. A good covering letter says that you are organised, logical and know what value you will bring to the table. Using the 'mirror technique' demonstrates a logical mind, a mature understanding of what the recruiter is looking for and the key thing the hirer needs to know at this stage which is, do you have the experience for the job so that I can invite you in for interview?

32. CVs/résumés

Your CV **(also referred to as a résumé)** is a vital tool in your job search armoury. It is your chance to sell yourself and your skills in a clear, simple, interesting and impactful way. A well-written CV will help you get an interview, focus the interviewer on your pertinent achievements and give them a clear overview of what you could do in this role for the hiring organisation.

If you are sending your CV in response to an advertisement, especially in a market where that role may get many responses, your

CV and cover letter may get no more than a cursory look. An interviewer will usually have three different piles they will separate the CVs into:

- the interview pile (CVs that look promising and highlight achievements matching the job specification);
- the hold pile (CVs that have potential if there are not enough candidates in the interview pile);
- the reject pile (CVs who do not hold the attention of the interviewer).

Your aim with both your CV and cover letter is to get into the interview pile! It is important that you stand out. We have set out below some key criteria that we know are effective in achieving this.

Compiling your CV

To make the recruiter's life easier, if you are sending your CV by email you should save it in a Word document as your full name. If you are going to change it, attach different version numbers to it e.g. Andrew_SmithCV1.doc. That way, if a company rings you once they have had your CV for a while, you can check which version they have and send them an updated copy. Again, it may seem obvious, but also don't password protect your CV! Unless you are an incredibly compelling candidate that the recruiter has heard of, it is more likely that someone will delete your CV than come back to you to ask you for the password.

A good rule of thumb for candidates is that if you have less than five years' experience you should be able to get your CV on to one page, those with more experience will probably need two pages. Even those with many years of experience should be aiming for two pages with three as an absolute maximum as their earlier career history is unlikely to be as relevant to the role they are applying for so can be summarised. The only true variation to this is for academics whose CVs are traditionally longer with a full list of published articles etc. Recruiters are most interested in what you have been doing for the last five years in detail so make sure this is what you emphasise; just writing a couple of bullet points for a position you were at for the last four years is not helpful.

Different parts of the world have slightly different formats or idiosyncrasies. More information on this can be found at **www.goingglobal.com** which sells guides on job hunting for specific countries. The most common CV we see and which is accepted by major companies worldwide is a reverse chronological CV. This means your experience is displayed with your most recent roles first.

It sounds obvious but all your CV needs to do is 'make it to the interview' pile, however, often people try and do too much with their CV believing it will get them the job.

Here are our top CV secrets which we've gathered over the years with the assistance of leading global recruiters, HR professionals and line managers responsible for hiring:

1. Make sure your CV has achievements as well as responsibilities listed and that these are evidence based.

Is there some evidence you can point to that proves you have the experience and the skills for the role you are applying for? Where possible start your bullet points with 'action verbs' e.g. initiated, managed, presented, led.

Achievements are key in deciding between candidates and are often missed out. If you consider two managers of Manchester United Football Club, Sir Alex Ferguson and Ron Atkinson, both had the same job responsibilities, but had a very different list of achievements.

2. Always write in the past tense not using the word 'I'

E.g. 'Achieved a 30 per cent increase in sales in the first six months by developing existing accounts.'

Rather than:

'I was a member of a team involved in developing existing accounts.'

3. Use a profile with caution

A profile is a paragraph, often at the top of a CV, which positions you in the eyes of the reader. It highlights key selling points or makes clear any ambiguity in your experience.

The jury is out about whether interviewers read these profiles – some like them, some are ambivalent, so unless it really adds something to your CV leave it out. Too many profiles are full of phrases such as 'brilliant communicator' or 'good team player'. These words may be true but they are only your opinion and not backed up by hard evidence, so effectively they are worthless statements! When you are making statements, especially in a profile at the beginning of your CV, make them objective rather than subjective – the reader should be able to look through your CV and find evidence to back up each of your claims.

Here is an example of a profile for a career changer (charity sector to commercial sector) which wasn't working:

'I have a strong track record of working in challenging situations; understanding and meeting the needs of diverse stakeholders and delivering results. My strengths are in analysis, persuasion and leadership. I believe my MBA has further developed my business skill set and will enable me to make a significant contribution in the demanding, fast-paced marketing position I seek. I am a dynamic communicator who is always respected by the teams I have worked with.'

And one that was on a CV which secured an interview:

'MBA marketing graduate with 10 years' experience of managing "charity brands". Extensive experience of running international teams of over 30 permanent and volunteer staff, managing key change programmes and communicating with key stakeholders.'

As you can see in the second example, the candidate positioned himself with greater clarity. He explained his background to a reader, highlighting the skills relevant to the job he was applying for, and used more evidence than the first candidate.

If you do use a profile, we suggest that it is no more than three or four lines long and that it is a good overview of you and your skills. It should also highlight the particular skills that you have that are identified as important to the role you have applied for. It can be a good way to ensure that the reader is in no doubt that you match all of the key requirements they are looking for.

4. Use bullet points to make your CV easy for the reader to scan your experience

Long paragraphs are hard on the eye making it difficult to pick out the relevant experience.

5. For everything you put on your CV ask yourself – so what?

You need to be able to justify in your own mind everything on your CV, so when you put down a bullet point, ask yourself, So what? What was achieved? What did that action lead to?

There is no rule to say you have to put down all your responsibilities and achievements so decide which are most relevant to the job you are applying for. You may have several CVs for different job applications that cater for this.

If you include them, what do your interests say about you? Typical endurance events such as marathons show persistence and resilience, for example. While interests are not recruitment criteria, they could make a difference if there are similar candidates and by giving some indication as to how you might fit in with the culture of the firm. Camilla was down to the final two for a role in banking and the line manager eventually offered her the role because she played the cello and so did he – he said that he couldn't split the candidates in any other way and thought they might at least have something in common!

6. The first two bullet points position you

Make sure you prioritise your bullet points and take particular care over which bullet points come first as the first two really position you to the reader.

7. The presentation of your CV is important

When you are preparing your CV in terms of its layout, make sure:

- The font is readable (font size should be no less than 10.5) and the layout is uncluttered with plenty of white space. This will make your CV much easier to read.
- Use bullet points rather than paragraphs of text.
- Keep your bullet points short and to the point.
- Spell check and then get a pedantic friend to read through your CV, checking and double checking for any spelling or grammatical errors.
- If your CV runs to more than one page, put your name and contact details in a footer on all pages so that if the front page should get separated, the company can still get hold of you.
- If you are sending your CV in hard copy, use white paper and don't use a binder or staples to keep it together. A recent candidate sent in his CV on neon paper which he said he hoped would make it stand out – it did, in the reject pile.
- In some parts of Europe, it is more common to use a photograph on a CV, but in the UK we would not recommend attaching a photo. Again, it is worth researching the accepted format in your location.

8. Always be honest

Never lie about your experience, qualifications or indeed anything on your CV – we have seen many examples where what a candidate thought was a fairly minor lie has led to job offers being revoked. It is not worth the risk and any lie that is discovered will cast you in a negative light.

9. Your CV should reflect you

When you have written your CV, have a final read through and check that it reflects you well and you are comfortable with it. It is your marketing document and so it is important that you are pleased with it. There are CV writing services available on the market but we advise our clients to stick with writing their own for a couple of reasons. Firstly, the CV writer will never truly know you and your experience as well as you do and a small change of nuance through lack of understanding can be important. Secondly, good recruiters can often spot when the CV has been written to a format by someone else (some can even tell which firm has written the document) and are often not flattering about the results.

10. Use a professional email address

When you put your contact email address on your CV ask yourself whether the address itself looks professional. We have seen so many which have been nicknames (often borderline inappropriate) and do not give the right impression. It is so easy to start a new email address, if in doubt, use an email address with your name in some format.

It may take several attempts to get your CV as you would want it but it is worth persevering.

Bear in mind that you may need several versions of your CV for the different job targets you are pursuing.

CVs for career changers

Career changers are typically unable to show experience in their target field and so relying on their CV to do the work for them is difficult. As you will have read in the networking section, most opportunities for career changers will be discovered by meeting people and proposing how you might be able to use your skills to add value to their organisation. For example, you can't hide the fact that you are a teacher and you now want to be a marketing manager but what you can do is show very clearly your transferable skills.

Some career specialists, and indeed some of our clients, have had success with functional CVs; this is when you state your transferable skills as a heading and then list below the evidence of these skills.

Sometimes this isn't possible as you may have had several jobs in which case you may want to list your transferable skills up front and then provide a reverse chronological summary of your employment history. The downside of this approach is that it makes it difficult for an employer to understand where in your employment your transferable skills were gained.

We prefer the more up front approach of listing your experience like a standard reverse chronological CV but clearly emphasising your transferable skills in each bullet point.

One key tip for career changers' CVs is to remove jargon. This is especially true if you are trying to break into a different industry or function as you will need to make sure that what you have done to date is understandable to this new audience. Some organisations have a raft of in-house jargon which is not easily understandable and if you have been using it for a while, you may not notice it anymore. Similarly if you use specific technical language remember that it is often not understood outside that field. If in doubt, give your CV to someone outside your industry and ask them whether it is clear what you do.

33. Interviews

'It's the first impression and will either open the door or close it.'

NICHOLAS SPARKS, American author

If everything has gone to plan, your covering letter and CV have been compelling and you have been invited in to meet an interviewer. Unfortunately, interviewing is not an exact science. Very few people are ever trained to conduct interviews and you may come across someone who only talks about themselves and hardly asks you any questions or you may find someone who has a list of questions they want to get through but no real sense of why they are asking them. It often helps if you work on the basis that it is your job to do the interviewer's job for them. If you know the skills and competencies they are looking for, rather than waiting for the interviewer to enquire about them, highlight them in your answers during your time together. It is up to you to get your message across.

Not all interviews are about getting the job – some may be just to screen out unsuitable candidates or to reduce the number of applicants to a manageable selection to be introduced to the manager who will decide on who gets the job. Knowing the purpose of your interview can be useful in how you structure your answers.

Over the years we have seen interviewees fall into some common traps that can count against them in their job search. We have set out below a number of those traps and some interviewing etiquette in the hope that you can avoid mistakes and show yourself to be a prime candidate.

There are plenty of books on self-branding if you want some detailed advice in this area but the key to it is to think carefully about how you present yourself. We have seen many younger people fall into the trap of not looking professional enough and older people coming across as old fashioned and stuck in a time warp! How you look will affect how you feel about yourself and whether you radiate confidence. As a general rule we recommend that you err on the side of dressing conservatively unless you are going to an interview in the creative industries. For women, dressing for interview is slightly trickier as they have to look professional but also 'up to date', perhaps wearing an accessory or two to show a little individuality. The most important thing is that you inspire confidence. Uncared for nails or scruffy shoes do little to promote this image; it is more important that you are remembered for what you say rather than what you wore.

We may as well start with the obvious things. It is always surprising how many candidates are late for interview. Get there early – being late because of traffic just doesn't cut it. And we know this is probably too much information, but if you use the bathroom before your interview – always wash your hands before you leave. Over the years, we have heard too many interviewers complain (particularly the men!) that they have just seen someone not wash their hands and they know that they are going to be the next to shake hands with them.

The reception area of a company has caught many a candidate out as they are observed chatting on their mobile phone by the interviewer. In the reception area you can learn quite a lot about a company. What is the vibe? Is it upbeat and positive? Do employees look happy and engaged or does everyone look like the grim reaper is just around the corner? Also, this is a place where people can learn about you so take the time to be nice to the receptionist and whatever you do don't chat inappropriately on your mobile phone – you never know who is listening!

First impressions

First impressions are incredibly important and in the first few seconds of meeting you interviewers are making their mind up about you – just as you do, when you are introduced to someone new.

It is important to try and be yourself as far as possible in interviews so that the interviewer can truly assess whether you will be a good fit in a particular role. If you are an introvert, don't try to come across as a party-loving extrovert. A recruiter it not only looking for someone with the right skills and experience for a role, they are also looking for a good match to the team or environment that the person will be joining. Although it may seem counterintuitive, try to avoid the mindset that it is more important to be offered the job than being offered the *right* job – you may end up kicking yourself if you find yourself in the wrong job in the wrong team.

Preparation before an interview is vital and will give you an edge – don't just have a quick look at the company's website (everyone will have done that). Who are their competitors? What did their most recent press release say? Is it relevant? What trends have you noticed in the industry?

Building rapport with the interviewer is always helpful – we are all human and if we like the person sitting opposite us, we are more likely to be well-disposed towards them. How can you do that? Make eye contact – we find that many people we interview will look almost anywhere other than at us! Smile, not all the time and, use your common sense – smiling when you are talking about making a team redundant doesn't make sense – engage with the person you are with by smiling at appropriate times. Try and match their conversational style – if they are very to the point, try and match that and make your answers more succinct and clear. If they tend to tell more of a story when they are talking, try and do the same.

Don't assume that the person interviewing you has read your CV or has been briefed on your abilities. It is important to create opportunities to sell yourself and highlight why you and your previous experience are key to the role. Don't presume that because it is on your CV that they are aware you are perfect for the job.

Never forget that an interview is a two-way process – having done all the hard work on establishing what you are looking for in your next role, bear this in mind when you are being interviewed. Is this really the role for you? Could you work in this environment? It is also important that you listen to the interviewer and show your interest by asking them questions that arise from their description of the role or about the company. You may well identify potential problem areas for the company which you have experience of tackling.

It may seem obvious but your attitude when you go into the interview will often determine the outcome. If you go into the interview with the belief you will be invited back for the next interview or offered the job, you are far more likely to be successful. If you think you are unlikely to get through, guess what…you're probably right.

General questions

While you can't prepare for every question you are going to get asked, it is worth being prepared for some of the more common ones:

- Tell me about yourself/talk me through your CV.
- Why are you applying?
- Why are you the best candidate for this role?
- Why do you want to leave your present employer?
- If I rang your boss for a reference, what would he or she say?
- Why would we hire you?
- How long will it take you to make a contribution?
- What interests do you have outside work?
- What has been your biggest achievement in your last role? In your life?
- What is your biggest weakness?
- What do you know about us?

One of the first things you may get asked is, 'so tell me about yourself'. This is your chance to sell yourself and deliver a clear, articulate 'elevator' pitch. It is very easy to fall into the trap of being too long winded but an 'elevator' pitch is essentially your opportunity to talk about yourself in an engaging and positive way in the time it takes to go from the ground floor to the top floor in an elevator.

Like your CV, it is useful to start with your education and work your way forward to your career explaining why you have made the decisions you have (why did you take your university course, go into a particular career etc.). If you have seen an advert or specification for the job you are being interviewed for, you will have a list of the core skills and competencies that are required. When you are talking about your career to date, try and highlight those skills and your experience, setting the scene that you have what they are looking for. Remember to bring the recruiter right up to date and explain why you are looking for a new role and why you are particularly interested in this role.

List below what you think are your three Unique Selling Points (USPs) and practise weaving them into your elevator pitch.

1.

2.

3.

You **will** get questions which are hard to answer. Bear in mind that sometimes the interviewer is interested in how you answer the questions when you don't know the answer as well as when you do! Can you think on your feet?

If there is a particular question that you really don't want to answer (e.g. why you didn't go to university, why you left a job etc.), it is worth having an answer prepared that you are reasonably happy with. We usually find that when you are prepared, the question never arises, and when you're not, you can count on it making an appearance. We have also seen many people start waffling when it comes to things they don't want to talk about and, bizarrely, they will then talk for far longer on the one thing they don't want to highlight on their CV. Be prepared and it will feel so much easier.

It is always the best policy to be honest but also to be upbeat and positive. Most people dread the question 'What is your biggest weakness?'. Pick a weakness that isn't a deal breaker – you don't want to totally rule yourself out of the job! Choose something you are working on or have improved recently, for example your presentation skills, which you could say you are actively working on and have recently joined a public speaking organisation (as long as you have!), to practise this skill.

Take some time to answer questions you find difficult – it is far better to take a few moments to gather your thoughts than rush into giving an ill-thought out answer or run the risk of giving an answer that goes on too long and is unstructured. Tips for buying some time are taking a breath, doing the 'thinking pose' where you show in your facial expression that you are thinking or use filler phrases such as 'let me think about the best example of that'.

We often get asked how long you should talk for when answering a question and as a general rule, between two and three minutes per answer is probably long enough. If your answer is necessarily longer, keep an eye on the interviewer and whether they are still with you – if in doubt, break the answer down into parts and ask if they have any questions.

Avoid jargon and keep your answers clear and simple – being too technical or going into too much detail can mean that your main points get lost.

Competency-based questions

Many companies now recruit against competencies. This means they will have a list of specific 'soft skills' or attitudes they are looking for. For example:

- ability to handle pressure;
- strong interpersonal skills;
- good communication skills.

These are attributes which are hard to find evidence of from a CV. In this type of interview, interviewers are trying to gather evidence by way of examples from your experience. You can tell if a question is a competency-based question if it references your past – so it may start with the words, 'Tell me about a time when…' or 'Describe a situation when…'.

We have found that the **STAR** format is very effective in giving a complete answer to these types of questions, which is why we have used this format in the skills exercise in Part Two.

S – What **situation** was this?
T – What was the **task** you had to perform?
A – What was the **action** that you took?
R – What was the **result** that you got?

Some competencies are specific to the role and some to the company. A recruiter is likely to have a list of these competencies which he or she will work through in the interview, trying to gather evidence for each one.

The job specification often details the competencies being sought for the role. Sometimes company-specific competencies can be found on the company's website e.g. in a list of 'core values' or in a mission statement. Once you have an idea of the competencies you will need to demonstrate, refer back to the results of the 'skills exercise' in Part Two. Decide which examples would best demonstrate the competencies you think they might be looking for. The knowledge you gain about yourself from the skills exercise will make it much easier to answer even the most unlikely competency-based questions.

Be aware that you may also get asked situational based questions where you have to describe how you have dealt with a specific situation e.g. how you managed an underperforming team member.

Questions for you to ask

Crucially, as we stated in Part Three, the questions you ask at interview are a strong indication of how much research you have done on the company and how seriously you are taking the interview. Don't ask questions which can be found out on the Internet but ones that are more subjective.

Example questions are:

- Why is the job open?
- Why did you join this company?
- What would my first assignment be?
- What are the development plans for the role/department?
- In your opinion, who will be the company's competitors in the future?
- Who would I be reporting to?

If you are at the beginning of the interview process (most companies will do more than one interview to recruit for a role), ask questions that will give you additional insight to build upon at subsequent interviews. This will give you an edge over other applicants as you will appear more knowledgeable.

> Tammy was a recruiter at an investment bank and says the questions the applicants asked at the end of the interview process were as important as the questions they answered during it, as they demonstrated the depth of research a candidate had gone into and whether they were serious about the company and the position.

Common interview mistakes

We find that that the same mistakes crop up again and again. The main ones are:

- Not having done enough research on the company or the industry as a whole. This shows a lack of interest and enthusiasm.

- Not listening to the question or answering a question you wish the interviewer had asked. This may work for politicians but won't work in a job.
- Providing too much information. Try to make sure that the information you are giving is relevant, succinct and to the point whilst still highlighting the important pieces of the story.
- Negotiating your salary before you've been offered the job.
- Criticising your current or previous employer.
- Focusing only on what you will get out of the role (promotion, higher salary etc.) – the focus should be on what you can do for them.
- Highlighting negatives when the question hasn't asked for it.

Assessment centres

Assessment centres are usually used to test and observe groups of candidates to see if they match the requirements of the role(s) being recruited for. They are generally run by experienced professionals who do this regularly and you will usually be briefed in advance on what to expect.

Interviews, personality questionnaires, group exercises, individual presentations, role plays and in-box exercises, (an in-box exercise requires a candidate to show how they would deal with typical items in an inbox/in-tray and is used to assess how they prioritise, plan, delegate and deal with the correspondence, memos etc they come across) as well as numerical and verbal reasoning tests, are the main selection tools used at assessment centres. You can't really practise group exercises and personality tests. It is better just to be yourself and to try not to second guess what they want. You can, however, practise for numerical and verbal reasoning tests, giving yourself a better chance of a higher score on the day. If you are keen to do some practice, you can find numerical and verbal reasoning tests at university careers centres or online. If you have an MBA you can revisit the work done in preparation for the GMAT test. These tests are very similar in content to the management-level tests you are likely to encounter at an assessment centre. You can also practise by paying to take a test online at **www.800score.com** or **www.gmac.com.**

When it comes to the other exercises involved during an assessment, be yourself – you want to be assessed on who you are not on who you think you should be.

Panel interviews

Occasionally you may face several interviewers (usually three or four) at once. This is particularly common in interviews for the public sector and you will usually be told that this is the case prior to the interview. If this is the first time you have faced a panel, it can be daunting, but everyone is in the same boat.

While addressing your answer to the person who asked the question, it is important to include the whole panel of interviewers in your answer, by glancing at them while you are answering the questions to make them feel included – as if you were telling a story to your friends but trying to impress one person the most!

You may get one of the interviewers asking really tough questions and one asking easy ones – this good guy/bad guy routine is designed to ruffle your feathers. Try to stay calm. Remember that you were asked to the interview because they thought you were a strong candidate for the job otherwise they wouldn't have wasted your time or theirs – they will be doing the same to all the candidates.

Telephone interviews

More and more interviews are now conducted initially by telephone to save on cost and time. We recommend the following:

- If possible, make sure you are on a landline in a quiet place to ensure there are no problems with reception or background noise.
- Vary the tone and pace of your voice to add interest.
- Tell the interviewer if you need some time to think through an answer. As before, phrases such as 'Let me think of the best example of that' are good fillers that buy you some time to think.
- Some candidates find standing up or talking in front of a mirror gives their voice more gravitas. It sounds a little odd but it really can work!

Follow-up letters

'The smallest act of kindness is worth more than the grandest intention.'
OSCAR WILDE, Irish writer and poet

After any meeting we recommend that you write a short follow-up letter, but after an interview it is particularly powerful. This letter can reiterate why you think you are the right person for the job. Often after a meeting you can think 'I wish I'd said that' or 'I wonder if they are concerned about this or that'. By writing a follow-up letter you give yourself the chance to address these issues. It shows you are interested in the job and gives the impression that you will be professional in following up with clients. Staying in touch with the company, even if you aren't successful, is a good way to stay on the radar, as the first choice candidate may turn down the role, not work out or, as in Louise's case, a new opportunity may open up within the company.

Louise signed up for job alerts from Guardian Jobs (online). This led her to apply for a position with a children's charity in the North – a regional office in Leeds. She wasn't offered the role but received positive feedback and was asked to stay in touch. She also signed up with several recruitment agencies in the not for profit sector. One of them contacted her to say that a suitable job was being advertised in the North West. It turned out to be the same job title/description as she had applied for previously but based at a different regional office at the children's charity. She thanked the recruiter but let them know that as she had applied to them directly on a previous occasion she couldn't let them work on her application from an ethical point of view. She then emailed the Head of Region in the North (Leeds) who had already interviewed her and asked that, if appropriate, could she refer her to the Head of Region in the North West (Manchester) which she did. And after another two rounds of interviews she got the job...So staying in touch and persistence worked.

Rejection

'I take rejection as someone blowing a bugle in my ear to wake me up and get going, rather than retreat.'
SYLVESTER STALLONE, American actor

Rejection is a component of the job search process and there is no getting away from it. We often find that a candidate will have put all their focus on one role and if they get rejected, find it hard to get motivated to start from scratch again. For that reason, we recommend that you have at least 10 opportunities that you are interested in (e.g. you have applied for the role) and aim for five opportunities that seem promising (e.g. you are at interview stage). So often, many of these opportunities will disappear through no fault of your own – the company has decided not to recruit after all, an internal candidate has been selected, and so on. If you have more options on the go, although you may be disappointed, you will have more positive avenues to pursue which can lessen the rollercoaster effect.

There is also an upside that most people don't consider. The interviewer may well have thought that your experience and skill set were the best but felt you would not fit into the team; they may well have saved you from a role you would have hated so perhaps a rejection can be a blessing in disguise.

If you do want to learn from the experience, you can contact the interviewer to ask for feedback. Be friendly and polite but don't push. Often they won't be able to give you useful feedback – it was a close run thing and they just felt the other candidate was a better fit – there was nothing you could have done better.

A positive mindset is vital especially after being turned down for a job. Watch the language you use – not, 'I'm not working', rather, 'I am considering several career options at the moment'. Mental health or state of mind is crucial when job hunting (and in life generally!). When you feel low and lack confidence you'll have worse days than when you feel confident and buoyant! Job hunting can be tough and so can changing career, but you are not alone – try to keep a sense of perspective. You can't work on your career or job hunt 24/7 – taking time off can make you more fired up when you return and you will appear more relaxed and 'less manic' at interview.

34. Negotiating the job and the salary

'Start out with an ideal and end up with a deal.'

KARL ALBRECHT, German entrepreneur who founded the Aldi supermarket chain with his brother Theo

If all goes well, you will start to receive job offers. It is, of course, the ultimate aim of any job search but it is also important not to leap in with both feet. When you get a job offer, it is important to consider whether it is the right job for you – are you accepting the job because it fits the criteria you have identified or just because it is a job and you are tired of the search? This is a good time to return to the matrix and see just how many of the points you have said are important to you it ticks. Are the areas where it does not match important enough to turn the job down or do you feel that the rest of the job is so interesting that you are willing to do without a particular aspect?

Once you've decided that it is the job for you – you are on to the negotiation phase of the process.

Negotiating

It's always a good idea to negotiate the job first and the salary second. Early on in the recruitment process we suggest that you are vague about your salary requirements by giving a broad-brush figure. If you are pushed into stating a salary then a good response is 'I'm looking for the market rate for this type of job', or, depending on how much knowledge you have you could say, 'Until I know more about the role it is difficult to know'. If you are asked directly for the figure that you earn now then you will have to give one. Don't forget to add in all the benefits you receive as this can inflate the overall figure.

If you are due a salary review soon you can also take this into account and disclose this to your interviewer. If you feel your salary doesn't reflect what you are worth now, perhaps you have just invested in an MBA for example, the best way to negotiate salary is to focus on how well you meet the requirements and what value you could add to the company. Try to generate as many job opportunities as possible – you are likely to come across as more confident at interview if you have options. If you are desperate because this job offer is the only one you have, that is hard to hide. It also weakens your position.

Giving the impression you are actively on the market with several options open to you gives the impression you are a good candidate and this means it is far more likely you will be offered a salary commensurate with the position. It's a game and if a company thinks that this is your only option you may be offered a low salary. If you give the impression you have some other serious options, the company will be more likely not to 'push its luck' and offer a higher salary to secure you.

Getting the timing right

We recommend that you don't start to negotiate the salary until you have had an offer from the company, ideally in writing. If you state a salary that is too low or too high you can put yourself out of the game without discussing and negotiating the job.

If the offer is below market level you either need to renegotiate the job, because if the job content changes the more likely it is that the salary level can be negotiated or you can negotiate what you feel is a fairer market rate. You should be able to find out what the market rate is by asking relevant recruitment agencies, looking on job advertisements, checking out salary studies in professional journals and making some discreet enquiries in your network, for example, by asking contacts for salary bands. Basic salary is not the only area you can negotiate on; you may be able to negotiate on benefits or perhaps more regular salary reviews. We have had clients negotiate equity stakes in a company as a way to get round a lower initial starting salary in a start-up company. Others have decided they would prefer to negotiate to reduce their working week by a day or include executive coaching in their salary package. Of course this all depends on the currency of your skills in the marketplace and the economic climate, which is why it is a good idea to regularly assess your worth within your industry.

Fiona interviewed for a senior IT role within a bank. She was overqualified for the role but the bank offered her a salary which did not take into account her additional experience. Fiona asked for another meeting with the decision makers (the IT Director and the CEO) and renegotiated the role to include more responsibility which she clearly had the experience to deliver. Given the increased remit of the role, when Fiona asked for a much increased salary, the company agreed and effectively created a new role for her with a salary 20 per cent higher than the salary they offered her initially.

35. The first 100 days

'Life is a great big canvas, and you should throw all the paint on it you can.'

DANNY KAYE, American actor and dancer

When you start in a new job, you are going to go through a considerable amount of change which starts when you accept the job offer and usually continues until about three months after you've started the new role.

Having an action plan to hit the ground running can considerably ease that period of change. You will never have a second chance to make a first impression so here are some aspects of a new role you may want to think about at key stages to make the best of the first three months in your new job.

Before you start

- Is there any additional research you can do about the company, your close colleagues or the industry that would be helpful prior to joining?
- How do you want to be perceived in the new business?
- Do you know how the company/your new boss will assess how well you are settling into your new role?

First month

- Do you have a clear understanding of reporting lines and the expectations your new boss/the company have for you? Are they achievable?
- Is the job as you expected or do you need to re-evaluate how you approach the job?
- Do you have an action plan for the first three months? What do you want to achieve? How do you want to be perceived?
- What 'early wins' can you work on to show your value to the company?
- Depending on your level of seniority, do you know the company strategy?
- Are there any influential people you have met who might act as mentors as you embed yourself in the company?
- When you first start, watching, listening and learning can be very useful as a strategy. Who are the real decision makers? What is the culture like, both formal and informal? Whose opinions count most in decision making?
- Don't be tempted to respond to negative comments from new colleagues. Find out the lay of the land before you weigh in with your opinion.

Third month

- Is the role progressing as expected? If not, what can you do to get it back on track?
- Do you have an action plan for the rest of the year?
- When will your performance be assessed? Do you know what you are being assessed against? Are there any areas you need to work on to ensure that the assessment is beyond expectations?

The important thing to remember is that getting the job is not where the career strategy ends. The most successful individuals are constantly looking at how they can deliver better and develop faster than their peers. You can do the same.

36. Long-term career management

'If you don't have a plan for yourself, you'll be part of someone else's.'
American proverb

You can't tell what will happen in the future and we all have to be flexible to changing circumstances. Knowing yourself and what you want goes a long way to carving out a satisfying and successful career. Having this knowledge helps you avoid career cul de sacs and recognise opportunities when you see them.

A couple of our clients go through the process outlined in the book but don't make any changes; perhaps they will come back to it in the future. Even if you never take it any further at least you know you have considered the options and made a conscious decision not to take action.

One of the biggest changes in the job market in the last 25 years is that the concept of a job for life is becoming increasingly rare. There is an expectation that people will now manage their own careers, looking for opportunities to develop with a base plan of what they want to achieve and where they want to go in terms of their work life. In reality, most people drift into a career almost by default – a comment from a teacher, parent or family friend who suggests that a certain job might suit their skills – and then find themselves on a conveyor belt that involves a promotion, the occasional new job when either they are forced to move (redundancy) or feel they need a change or salary rise. Usually, very little strategic thinking goes into those decisions or whether the direction in which they are moving, and felt was right early in their career, is now appropriate. What we hope is that this book will encourage you to become more strategic about your own career.

From the moment you start earning your own living, you are effectively running your own consultancy company and need to have a strategy that responds to market changes, your values and your needs (financial and otherwise). Any good company would review this on a regular basis; your consultancy 'clients' are your employers – you are there to do a piece of consultancy work for them. When you or they feel that that value has passed, you move on.

AVRIL MILLAR CASE STUDY

I graduated from Glasgow University in the very early 1970s as a civil engineer, which was extremely unusual in those days. Indeed, so odd was it that applications for jobs returned with requests for photographs before interview. However, I did get work – not sure what that says about my looks, the quality of the photograph or the curiosity of the employers! My first job was in the Corporation of Glasgow Sewage Department but my husband was in the RAF and we moved to Malta not long afterwards; my engineering career was cut short.

When my children were three and five years old, I was living in the far north of Scotland and travelled daily from Forres to Aberdeen to do my PGCE. I then taught physics for several years, ending up teaching Oxbridge entrance. I quit teaching in 1986, having decided that much as I loved the subject and the students, I may well end up in prison for manslaughter due to the sheer boredom of the staffroom. As I was Head of Department, I had to give two terms' notice, which I thought was more than sufficient time for a talented, intelligent 35-year-old to find work. Nope.

I fell into financial services in 1986 and spent the first year hating every minute of it. Those were the days of 'rape and pillage' in the financial world so I left and went self-employed, finally setting up my own wealth management firm, in which I was involved until the end of 2006.

I then qualified as a Master Practitioner of NLP, a Personal, Executive and Business Coach and a Master Hypnotherapist which led to me doing a great deal of executive and business coaching and, as a result I was asked by one of my coachees to run his headhunting business in the City. I have now set up another business training ex-City and corporate people to work with SMEs, helping them to grow faster and more sustainably and profitably. I also retain two non exec positions in the City, one in the headhunting business and one with a financial trading business. I also have a modest but hopefully growing career in speaking and writing. I am 57, in case anyone out there thinks it's too late to do anything.

Key impacts on your long-term career management strategy

As you navigate your career and keep an eye on where your industry/career is going in the future you should consider:

- **New employment trends.**
- **Keeping your skills up to date – it is important to consider what training you need to get to the next level in your career.**
- **Your changing circumstances – whether intentional or inadvertent, there is one thing you can count on – your life will change.**

It is well worth reviewing your matrix once a year to see if what you are looking for in a role/career is still the same or if your requirements are changing. Perhaps you now have children and work/life balance is more of a priority or perhaps global travel is not quite the draw it once was. If there are substantial changes to your needs – can you make changes to your existing role to take these into account or is now the time to start thinking about a new role or direction?

If you don't have a career strategy, what can you do today to start formulating one? Is there anything in your aspirations for the future that will give you a starting point? Perhaps it would be worth drawing up an action plan to create some momentum.

After completing this process, if it's not now, then at the very least you will have a plan so you know when, it will make your current position more bearable knowing there is an end goal in sight.

FINAL THOUGHTS

'There's no such thing as too late.
That's why they invented death.'
From the movie *Out to Sea*

Having been through this process ourselves and then helped our clients navigate this methodology, we are keen to share what we have learnt over the last 20 years as both recruiters and as career coaches. Many people find the process hard work and some will not put in sufficient effort to reap the rewards, but we hope we have done enough through the book and with the case studies to show just what is possible if you keep going, even when it gets tough. The rewards really are worth the effort.

Without a doubt this process takes time and effort but as our clients testify it is fulfilling to have a career that you are engaged with and enjoy. You can tell at interview those candidates who have a real passion and interest in their work; their eyes shine and they have more energy. We believe life is too precious not to make the most of your working life and we have given you in this book everything we have learnt (from our own, and our clients' experiences) about how to navigate your career.

This is the book that we both wish we had had when we started trying to carve out a more satisfying career. The idea for writing this book came about when we were discussing what we could do to strengthen our own careers, i.e. career strategising! We were lucky enough, through networking, to find a publisher who liked what we had to say (thank you Lisa and her team!) and we hope that, as you work your way through the book, you will realise what your options are and feel encouraged to make a start on your career change. We hope, too, that the stories of our clients will inspire you to fulfil your potential in work and in life generally – enjoy the journey!

APPENDIX: REFERENCES AND RESOURCES

Books often have very large reference and resource sections and you are left no wiser as to which information source to choose from a very long list. We would rather guide you to the books which we and our clients have found particularly helpful.

We have chosen our references and resources sparingly to focus on what we feel will be the most useful for you.

Part One: If not now, when? What's holding you back?

Time management

Tracy, Brian. *Eat That Frog! Get more of the important things done, today!* London: Mobius, 2004.

Overcoming fear

Jeffers, Susan. *Feel the fear and do it anyway.* London: Vermilion, 2007.

Johnson, Spencer. *Who Moved My Cheese? An amazing way to deal with change in your work and in your life.* London: Vermilion, 1999.

Taking a step into the unknown

Goddard, Gabriella. *Gulp! The seven-day crash course to master fear and break through any challenge.* London: Penguin, 2006.

Part Two: Understanding yourself and what you want

Career tests

Tieger, D. Paul and Barron-Tieger, Barbara. *Do What You Are: Discover the perfect career for you through the secrets of personality type.* London: Little, Brown and Company, 2007.

Passmore, Jonathan. *Psychometrics in Coaching: Using psychological and psychometric tools for development.* London: Kogan Page, 2008.

Defining your skills and strengths

Buckingham, Marcus, and Clifton, Donald O. *Now, Discover Your Strengths: How to develop your talents and those of the people you manage.* London: Pocket Books, 2005.

Your interests and passions

Sher, Barbara. *Refuse to Choose! A revolutionary program for doing everything that you love.* London: Rodale Books, 2007.

What do I want out of life? Defining your long-term plan

Turner, Colin. *Born to Succeed: Releasing your business potential.* London: Texere Publishing, 2002.

Canfield, Jack. *How to get from where you are to where you want to Be.* London: HarperElement, 2007.

Part Three: Now what? How to research, brainstorm and move forward

Setting up a business

Gerber, Michael E. *E-Myth Revisited: Why most small businesses don't work and what to do about it.* London: HarperCollins, 1994.

Part Four: Job search strategy – getting interviews and securing the job

Networking

D'Souza, Steven, *Brilliant Networking: What the best networkers know, say and do.* London: Prentice Hall, 2007.

Carnegie, Dale. *How to Win Friends and Influence People.* London: Vermilion, 2007.

Influencing

Cialdini, Robert. *Influence: The Psychology of Persuasion.* London: HarperBusiness, 2007.

CVs

Howard, Simon. *Creating a Successful CV.* London: Dorling Kindersley Limited, 1999.

Covering letters

Innes, James. *Brilliant Cover Letters: What you need to know to write a truly brilliant cover letter.* London: Prentice Hall, 2009.

Interviews

Yate, Martin John. *Great Answers to Tough Interview Questions.* London: Kogan Page, 2008.

Porot, Daniel and Bolles Haynes, Frances. *Best Answers to 202 Job Interview Questions: Expert tips to ace the interview and get the job offer.* London: Impact Publications, 2008.

Edenborough, Dr. Robert. *Brilliant Psychometric Tests: What the best candidates know, do and say.* London: Prentice Hall, 2009.

Portfolio working

Hopson, Barrie. *And What Do You Do? 10 steps to creating a portfolio career.* London: A & C Black, 2009.

First 100 Days

Watkins, Michael D. *The First 90 Days: Critical success strategies for new leaders at all levels* Boston: Harvard Business School Press, 2003.

Our website

Visit us at **www.howtotakechargeofyourcareer.com.**

Here we link to more books we have found useful but which are specific to a certain topic. The website is also where you can find downloadable blank forms for the exercises in the book.

BIBLIOGRAPHY

Ball, Ben. *Assessing Your Career: Time for change? (Personal and Professional Development)*. London: Wiley Blackwell, 1996.

Beckel, Heather. *Be a Kickass Assistant: How to get from a grunt job to a great career.* London: Headline, 2002.

Black, Roger. *Getting Things Done: A radical new approach to managing time and achieving more at work*. London: Penguin Group, 1987.

Boldt, Laurence G. *How to Find the Work You Love*. London: Arkana, 1996.

Bolles, Richard Nelson. *What Color is Your Parachute? 2010: A practical manual for job-hunters and career-changers.* London: Ten Speed Press, 2009.

Bolles, Richard Nelson. *The Job-Hunter's Survival Guide: How to find hope, and rewarding work even when 'There are No Jobs'*. London: Ten Speed Press, 2009.

Bolles, Richard Nelson and Figler, Howard. *The Career Counselor's Handbook*. London: Ten Speed Press, 1999.

Bronson, Po. *What Should I Do With My Life?* London: Vintage, 2004.

Carson, Richard D. *Taming Your Gremlin* Revised: *A surprisingly simple method for getting out of your own way.* San Francisco: HarperSanFrancisco, 2003.

Chan, James. *Spare Room Tycoon: Succeeding independently – the 70 lessons of sane self-employment*. London: Nicholas Brealey Publishing, 2000.

Coomber, Stephen, Crainer, Stuart and Dearlove, Des. *The Career Adventurer's Fieldbook: Your guide to career success.* London: Capstone Publishing Limited, 2002.

De Grunwald, Tanya. *Dude, Where's My Career? The guide for baffled graduates.* West Sussex: Summersdale Publishers, 2008.

Grigg, Joanna. *Getting into Self Employment.* London: Trotman & Co Ltd, 1999.

Green, Graham. *The Career Change Handbook: How to find out what you're good at and enjoy – then get someone to pay you for it.* Oxford: How To Books Ltd, 2008.

Guerriero, Janice, M. and Allen, Robert G. *Key Questions in Career Counselling – techniques to deliver effective career counselling services.* Philadelphia: Lawrence Erlbaum Associates Inc, 1998.

Hall, Richard. *The Secrets of Success at Work: 10 steps to accelerating your career.* London: Pearson Education Limited, 2008.

Handy, Charles B. and Handy, Elizabeth. *The New Alchemists.* London: Hutchinson, 2004.

Hawkins, Dr. Peter. *The Art of Building Windmills: Career tactics for the 21st century.* Liverpool: Graduate Into Employment Unit, 1999.

Hopson, Barrie and Scally, Mike. *Build Your Own Rainbow: A workbook for career and life management.* East Sussex: Management Books, 2009.

Hornby, Malcolm. *3 Easy Steps to the Job You Want.* London: Financial Times/Prentice Hall, 2000.

Jacobs, Richard. *What's Your Purpose? Seven questions to find your answer.* London: Mobius, 2004.

Katz, Margot. *Tarzan and Jane: How to thrive in the new corporate jungle.* London: Profile, 2007.

Klein, Steve. *Jobwise: 150 tips to help you survive and thrive in your career.* London: John Wiley & Sons, 2000.

Lees, John. *How to Get a Job You'll Love: A practical guide to unlocking your talents and finding your ideal career.* Berkshire: McGraw-Hill Professional, 2008.

Lore, Nicholas. *The Pathfinder, How to Choose or Change your Career for a Lifetime of Satisfaction and Success.* London: Simon & Schuster, 1998.

Marshall, Judi. *Women Managers Moving On: Exploring career and life choices.* London: Thomson Learning, 1995.

Messmer, Max. *Managing Your Career for Dummies.* London: IDG Books Worldwide Inc, 2000.

Nathan, Robert and Linda Hill (estate). *Career Counselling (Counselling in Practice series).* London: Sage Publications Ltd, 2005.

Nemko, Marty, Edwards, Paul and Edwards, Sarah. *Cool Careers for Dummies.* London: IDG Books Worldwide Inc, 1998.

Oates, David and Shackleton ,V.J. . *Perfect Recruitment: All you need to get it right first time.* London: Arrow Books Ltd, 1994.

Otterbourg, Robert K. *Switching careers.* Washington: The Kiplinger Washington Editors, 2001.

Porot, Daniel. *The Pie Method for Career Success: A unique way to find your ideal job.* Minneapolis: JIST Works, Inc, 1996.

Pink, Daniel H. *The Adventures of Johnny Bunko: The last career guide you'll ever need.* New York: Business Plus, 2008.

Prince, Jeffrey P. and Heiser, Lisa J. *Essentials of Career Interest Assessment (Essentials of Psychological Assessment).* London: John Wiley & Sons, 2000.

Pyke, Gary and Neath, Stuart. *Be Your Own Career Consultant: Where do you want to be?* London: Pearson Education Limited, 2002.

Robinson, Jonathan and Carmel, McConnell. *Un-Ltd: Tell me what is it you plan to do with your one wild and precious life.* London: Momentum, 2002.

Rowe, Dorothy. *The Successful Self.* London: HarperCollins, 1996.

Sher, Barbara and Smith, Barbara. *I Could Do Anything If I Only Knew What it Was: How to discover what you really want and how to get it.* London: Bantam Doubleday Dell Publishing Group, 1994.

Sinetar, Marsha. *Do What You Love, the Money Will Follow: Choosing your right livelihood.* London: Bantam Doubleday Dell Publishing Group, 1996.

Spillane, Mary. *Branding Yourself: How to look, sound and behave your way to success.* London: Sidgwick & Jackson, 2000.

Taylor, David. *The Naked Leader.* London: Capstone, 2002.

Taylor, Denise. *How to Get a Job in a Recession*. Canada: Brook House Press, 2009.

Taylor, Ros and Humphrey, John. *Fast Track to the Top: 10 skills for career success.* London: Kogan Page Ltd, 2001.

The Mind Gym. *Give Me Time.* London: Time Warner Books, 2006.

Tolle, Eckhart. *The Power of Now: A guide to spiritual enlightenment.* London: Mobius, 2001.

Wade, Sarah and Rice, Carole Ann. *Find Your Dream Job: True stories and proven strategies for getting a job you love.* London: Marshall Cavendish, 2009.

Waldroop, James and Butler, Timothy. *The 12 Bad Habits that hold Good People Back: Overcoming the behaviour patterns that keep you from getting ahead.* London: Broadway Business, 2001.

Wendleton, Kate. *Interviewing and Salary Negotiation: For job hunters, career changers, consultants and freelances.* New Jersey: The Career Press, 1999.

White, Kate. *Why Good Girls Don't Get Ahead but Gutsy Girls Do: Nine secrets every career woman must know:* New York: Grand Central Publishing, 1995.

Williams, Nick. *The Work We Were Born To Do: Find the work you love, love the work you do.* London: Element Books, 2000.

Winter, Barbara. *Making a Living Without a Job: Winning ways for creating work that you love.* London: Bantam Books, 1993.

Wright, Bridget. *Careershift: How to plan and develop a successful career.* London: Piatkus Books, 1999.

Yeung, Rob. *The Ten Career Commandments: Equip yourself with the 10 most important skills to move up the career ladder.* Oxford: How To Books Ltd, 2002.

INDEX